CORNBREAD & Collard Greens

How West African Cuisine & Slavery Influenced Soul Food

Deah Berry Mitchell

Photography by Thaddeus Jefferson

ISBN 978-1-970079-13-5

Library of Congress Control Number: 2019931456

Published and Edited: Opportune Independent Publishing Co.

Design, Layout and Photography by: Thaddeus Jefferson

113 N. Live Oak Street

Houston, TX 77003

(832) 263-1700

www.opportunepublishing.com

For more information about the author please visit and contact:

www.deahmitchell.com

CONTENTS

THE THING ABOUT RECIPES...

Soul food requires a certain level of confidence. Ask any good cook what their recipe is, and you'll likely find it hard to get a straight answer. That's because, for many of us, cooking is a pleasurable experience that requires creativity, intuitiveness and most importantly, the ability to follow your gut. A good cook will toss fragrant spices into a hot pan without second-guessing that it will be too much. What I love most about cooking is that it allows you to learn from your mistakes and that sometimes things can be salvaged. Cooking is a lot like life - it is all about balance. The sooner you realize that, the better off you'll be. Too salty? Add something sweet to balance. Once we learn how to properly balance flavors, the rest just falls into place.

Because we sometimes take for granted our ability to translate recipes in our heads onto a plate without written steps, I felt it necessary to include a visual aid as a reference for such commonly used words in cooking as "a pinch of..." "a heavy pinch..."

As with all recipes I recommend knowing your own palate and your preferences. My recipes are to be used as guides, however, if you prefer more salt or heat from peppers feel free to adjust as needed.

PREFACE

CORNBREAD & COLLARD GREENS

Today many dishes are still cooked and prepared the same way our parents and grandparents taught us, and the way their parents and grandparents taught them. Despite how diabetes, heart disease, and high cholesterol plague our African-American communities, little is said about the reasons we may be unwilling to depart from what modern medicine has declared our deadliest dietary habits.

Cooking and eating in our culture is more than merely a means of survival. We connect with family after church services by praying over a succulent ham and a mix of collards and turnips that have been simmering in a pot all day.

We celebrate a rousing game of spades or sometimes slam down the "bones" by yelling an enthusiastic "Domino!" while eating fried catfish and bright yellow potato salad. An endless train of sock-it-to-me cakes and chicken lines the kitchen tables of every family during repass. Maybe there is something much simpler that explains why we cannot seem to let go of these meals. Perhaps these old recipes and cooking techniques are one of the only ways descendants of slaves can continue their familial customs. These are our family crests, the last remaining connection to an otherwise tortured and broken lineage.

Both the traditional and contemporary food culture of modern African-Americans compared with the "typical" American diet is highly influenced by Africans, in particular West Africans.. The food tells a rich and poignant story of both endurance and adaptability during hard circumstances.

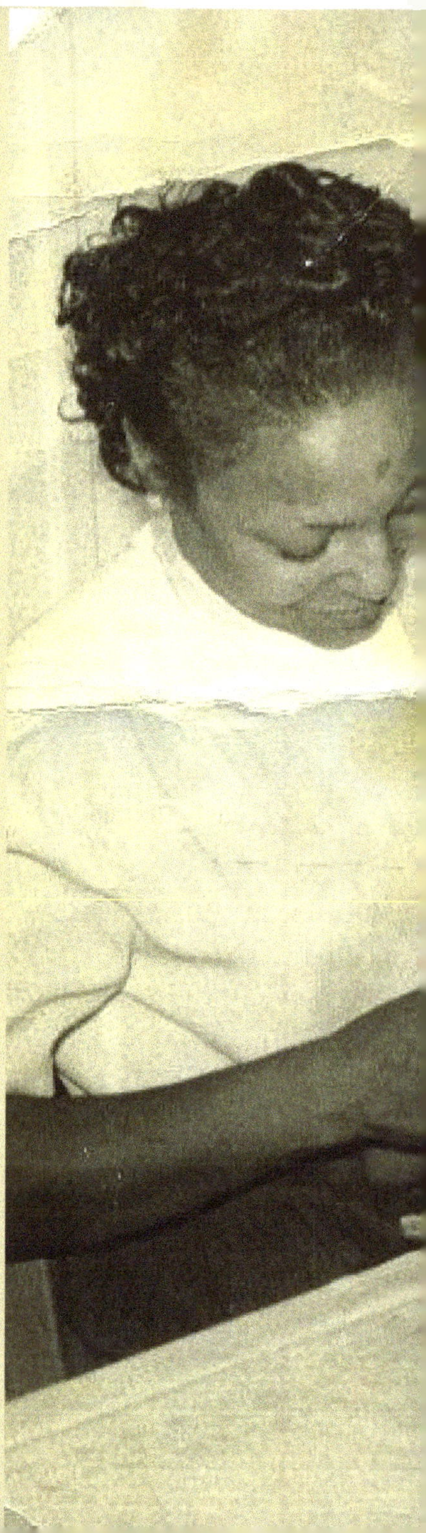

Kobe, Japan Circa 1954 - My dad as a baby.
Left to right; Grandmother, Mrs. Wilma "Pete" Berry,
my dad, Uncle James, Grandfather, Sargeant James Berry

These are a few of my favorite things…

I have two distinct food memories from my childhood that are equally formative to my adulthood. My first memory is single-handedly responsible for my love of all things breakfast and brunch. Growing up with a Southern maternal grandmother from East Texas and a contemporary mother who loved culture, breakfast was always a big deal in our home. It was not unusual for these doting women to prepare lavish breakfasts, not just on the weekends, but during the school week... Pork chops, eggs, bacon, homemade biscuits, creamy grits, hot-buttered pancakes, and homemade jellies were the norm.

But Sundays were by far my favorite. On Saturday nights, I would fall asleep in my grandmother's bed. I'd awaken the next morning to the sound of Gospel music blaring and the come-hither scent of fresh-brewed coffee and fanatically frying bacon. If I close my eyes, I can still hear the popping from the hot cast iron skillet my grandmother used for everything. The cast iron was not unusual, though some of her cooking techniques may have been unorthodox.

Sherman, Texas - Deah, Age 3
Me and my maternal grandmother Rosie Lee Lovelady Mitchell aka Bigmama

Bigmama would rest the greasy bacon on newspaper to drain while she wiped out the crispy remnants the pork had left behind. She would then place a tablespoon or so of butter into the bottom of the still-very-hot pan and watch it disappear. Finally, she'd delicately dip slices of white bread into the melted butter and proceed to fry it on both sides.

At home, we referred to this method as nothing more than just making toast. Thinking back, I don't think I had ever seen a toaster or even heard of one at this time. An electric gadget with heating elements inside that springs out crispy slices of bread? What kind of wizardry was that? Nope. I was perfectly satisfied with and preferred Bigmama's toast, slightly damp in the center from butter.

It was and still is the best way to eat toast in my opinion. To this day, I have never owned a toaster and it is because of Bigmama. I feel as though she's looking down from Heaven, proud of my decision to not cave into the pressures of the 21st century.

My second vivid memory of food involves dear ol' mom. My mother was a bit ahead of her time. When other friends would reluctantly run home for mundane dinners, my mom always made mealtime special. She was instrumental in teaching me to keep things exciting and step outside of my comfort zone. While my grandmother taught me to appreciate the traditional side of soul food, my mother taught me to expand my palate at a very young age.

One particular day, my mom was on her way home from lunch and stopped by a new deli in our hometown, called 'Vitina's Delights'. The restaurant's glowing red signage welcomed guests to try the freshly prepared deli sandwiches and salads. My mother brought home a paper bag and, upon leaving to return to work, left the contents with me.

I remember unwrapping the white butcher paper and ogling the artisanal bread, which hugged thinly sliced deli meats and fresh peppers. The sandwich was tangy from the vinegar and oil dressing, and the cheese— oh, that glorious cheese— was delightfully pungent. I fell in love instantly. It wasn't the boxed block of government cheese I had tasted before, thanks in part to my grandmother's subsidies. Nor was it like the plastic-wrapped cheese slices. Oh no! It had a much more mature flavor. Although I don't know the exact ingredients of the sandwich, its taste had a lasting impression on my budding culinary repertoire. I often credit this moment as my culinary and emotional awakening, when I decided to try new things in and out of the kitchen.

Sherman, Texas - Deah age 7
Me and mama

Just as my food memories are very much tied to my familial roots, so too are soul food and family recipes strongly intertwined with many other African-American families' recollections. Food has always played a major role in culture, but perhaps none more so than in the African-American community. Often, food is the only tangible connection to a history gripped in slavery. Something as seemingly insignificant as food serves as a historical roadmap from generation to generation. Both traditional and contemporary African-American food culture tells a rich and beautiful story of endurance and adaptability during hard circumstances, a story which I hope to interpret through personal narratives, research, and creative licenses.

WHAT TO EXPECT

This book contains three sections:
home, rations, and creativity.

- **HOME** - During the transatlantic slave trade, slaves brought over their knowledge of cooking techniques, meals, and ingredients.
- **RATIONS** - Rationed portions of foods were used as a form of control over slaves. As a result, slaves were forced to make do with small food portions and created dishes that are still cooked today.
- **CREATIVITY** - For generations, our culture has become synonymous with using our creative skills to enhance foods. Soul food has many influences from indigenous peoples, the British and the Carribbean.

My hope is that, on each page, you'll find something new and exciting about African-American culture, the contributions made by slaves, and, on a broader scale, how this cuisine has influenced Southern culture even today. The personal recipes I've included in this book are creative interpretations. In no way do I believe that my recipes are better or more dignified because I've opted to make something new out of traditional soul foods.

On the contrary, I like to think that my ancestors would be proud to know that I've been inspired and inherited the long-held tradition of recreating. Make no mistakes about it; no matter where I travel or what I cook in my kitchen, I am still the same little two-plait-wearing country girl who loves sitting on the front porch barefoot and eating soft crumbly cornbread mashed into ice cold sweet buttermilk, and slow-cooked collard greens with savory pot liquor (or pot likker). (I'll explain more on that combination on page 17.) In the meanwhile, devour this book, be inspired to find your own cooking "voice," and, most of all, enjoy this spiritual culinary journey–from West Africa over 400 years ago to your home today.

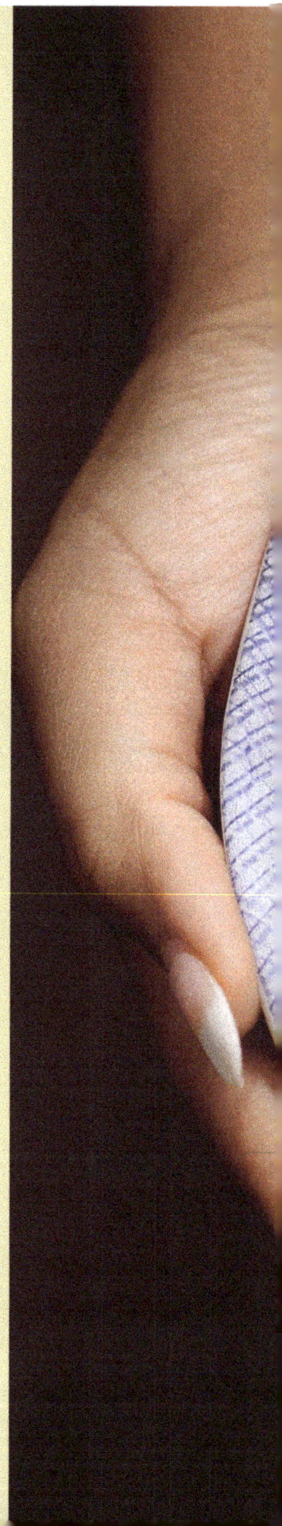

HOME

"Ulo" in Igbo

"If you watch your pot, your food will not burn."
—Nigerian Proverb

Coming from diverse regions and communities, West Africans adapted their cultures to the weather, resources, and restrictions they experienced in bondage. Enslaved black cooks filled North America's Southern landowner's platters and stomachs.

Many slaves passed through the West Indies while bound for America. Soon Southern plantations were feasting on spicy foods, cornbread, African vegetables, greens, pot liquor, and sweet potato puddings. In addition, they experienced different cooking techniques. Africans were known for grilling over open pits in the ground and deep fat frying. In their cuisine, cooks of African origin included black-eyed peas, hominy grits, okra, eggplant, melons, and sorghum (sometimes used as a richer, more concentrated-flavored substitute for honey). In West Africa and parts of Brazil, black-eyed peas are considered street food. These peas were brought from Africa to America, just like rice and gumbo. To make what West Africans called "Akara" and Brazilians call "Akarajé", black beans are peeled, mashed, rolled into balls, and fried into crispy little beignets, or bread. Many parts of Africa serve it the same way with hot sauce.

The following foods, meals, and/or cooking techniques were brought from West Africa during the transatlantic slave trade. Black-eyed peas, rice, yams, fried food technique, gumbo, Hoppin' John, okra, peanuts

Dishes found today in American and Caribbean cuisine like jambalaya, Hoppin' John (peas and rice), gumbo (made with okra) were variations and readoptions of foods found in West African countries such as Nigeria, Benin, Guinea, and Senegal. Quintessentially African dishes such as Jollof rice are likely predecessors to the creole prepared dish jambalaya. It is regionally specific, but one thing never changes…at its heart it is a hearty rice, tomato and tomato paste with spices made in one pot as a meal.

Black-eyed peas have established themselves as essential to the diet of all Southerners. They began as food for farm animals and were part of the rations fed to slaves. In the Black community, it has long been believed that black-eyed peas and greens should be consumed as a New Year's tradition to encourage good luck and prosperity. One common story believed by many to have started this tradition is the beans' resemblance to coins, and the greens symbolize paper currency.

As long as I can remember, my grandmother and mother passed down this culinary tradition for good luck. Full disclosure, I never liked black-eyed peas, but I absolutely loved greens...specifically collards. So, I wanted to think of a way to pay homage to black-eyed peas with a creative twist (pg. 18).

In the summers while my mother worked, I'd sit outside on the porch, and my grandmother would read the Bible to my cousins and I. Afterwards she fed us greens from her plate and would mix a somewhat unusual concoction of cornbread and buttermilk. She'd meticulously churn these two ingredients into a tall glass and then spoon-feed the glorious mush to me. It was sour, sweet, and filling at the same time. This very-Southern combination was my version of the tried and true peanut butter and jelly sandwich.

To this day, I think the perfect companion to greens is buttermilk. I created a collard green and black-eyed pea ravioli with buttermilk cream sauce as a comforting nod to my past, but I also wanted to show my expanding culinary skills. Homemade ravioli paired with two Southern classics and a béchamel sauce? Yes, please.

Freedman's Cemetery, Dallas, Texas

BLACK-EYED PEA AND COLLARD RAVIOLI WITH BUTTERMILK BÉCHAMEL SAUCE

Estimated Time: 1 hour
Servings: 4

Ravioli:

Ingredients–

See page 80 for ingredients/instructions for Easy Basic Pasta recipe

Filling:

2 TABLESPOONS OLIVE OIL

3-4 GARLIC CLOVES, CHOPPED

½ SMALL WHITE ONION, CHOPPED

1 CUP COOKED OR CANNED BLACK-EYED PEAS

1 BUNCH GREENS (15 LEAVES, STEM REMOVED) OR 1- 16OZ CAN OF GREENS

6 OUNCES GOAT CHEESE

12 OUNCES PARMESAN

1 TEASPOON NUTMEG

SALT AND PEPPER TO TASTE

How to make filling:

1. Heat a large pan and add olive oil, chopped garlic cloves, and onion.
2. Sauté until onion begins to sweat or become translucent. Next, add greens until completely wilted. Because collards have tough leaves, add about 1 cup of water and allow them to simmer for about 30-40 minutes. Drain any liquid off greens and add black-eyed peas. Mix thoroughly until well incorporated. Then, remove from heat.
3. Add goat cheese. Goat cheese should be room temperature, or you may soften by heating in microwave 10 seconds.
4. After mixing all of the ingredients together, add a dash of nutmeg to taste. Adding nutmeg may sound odd, but nutmeg and green leafy vegetables pair well together. Add salt and pepper to taste and then set the mixture to the side. Your filling should be fairly thick. If it is too runny, place the ravioli filling in t he refrigerator to firm up for up to 30 minutes.

Making the ravioli:

5. Lay one thin pasta sheet on a flat surface. The surface should be wide enough to make two large rows or three to four smaller rows (the rows will become guidelines to cut your ravioli).
6. Place about 2 teaspoons of filling on dough about 1 ½ to 2 inches apart, making sure not to overfill the scoop. Once the entire sheet is filled, place the second layer of pasta dough directly on top of the already-filled one and press gently. Press out any excess air. Use pasta roller or take a sharp knife and cut ravioli pieces out, or use a small biscuit cutter to press out circular ravioli. Set ravioli to side and begin making the sauce using the same pan you made ravioli filling in.

Creamy Buttermilk Béchamel Sauce

Ingredients–

½ CUP BUTTERMILK

¾ CUP HEAVY CREAM

¼ CUP WHITE WINE OR CHICKEN BROTH

1 LEMON, ZESTED

½ CUP BUTTER

3-4 TABLESPOONS FLOUR

3 TABLESPOONS PARSLEY

1. Heat skillet (same used for filling) on medium. Add butter, 2 tablespoons flour, and stir slowly until it starts to take form together. Add white wine or chicken stock to deglaze the pan. Then add salt and pepper to taste.
2. Add remaining flour, then slowly alternate adding buttermilk and cream while continuously stirring.
3. Once ingredients are combined and sauce begins to thicken, lower temperature to low heat setting and simmer for 2 minutes.
4. Add ravioli into sauce and continue to simmer an additional 5-7 minutes until the sauce and ravioli are mar ried and an indescribable aroma begins to permeate the air.
5. Turn off heat, remove pan from burner and add zest from 1 whole lemon and parsley before serving.

CREAMED COLLARD GREEN SOUP WITH CORNBREAD CROUTONS

Estimated Time: 1 hour and 10 minutes
Servings: 5-6

Ingredients-

1 CUP CHOPPED ONION

4 CHOPPED GARLIC CLOVES

3 SLICES BACON OR PANCETTA, COOKED AND CHOPPED

1 ½ CUPS CHICKEN BROTH OR VEGETABLE BROTH

½ CUPS WATER

2 CUPS HALF AND HALF OR CREAM

2 TABLESPOONS BUTTER

3 BUNCHES OF COLLARD GREENS OR 45-50 LEAVES (CLEANED AND CHOPPED)

1 TABLESPOON VINEGAR OR APPLE CIDER VINEGAR

1 TABLESPOON SALT

1 TEASPOON NUTMEG

How to prepare soup:

1. Add butter to pot and melt. Add chopped onion and garlic and pork until pork is fried.
2. Place greens into pot, followed by liquids.
3. Cook on medium heat for one hour and strain liquid, reserving pot liquor (remember: the liquid left behind after boiling greens or beans is often referred to as "pot liquor" in the South.) to add back later.
4. Put cooked greens into high powered blender. As you blend on high, slowly alternate adding 1 cup pot liquor to 1 cup cream until soup reaches your desired consistency. I prefer a thicker, creamy soup with "body"…in other words, when you stir with a spoon it will coat the back of the spoon and slowly slide off. If you prefer this thick, you will not use the enter cup of pot liquor. Lastly, add a drizzle (approximately 1 tablespoon) of olive oil to finish.
5. Top with a dollop of sour cream, pancetta bits, and cornbread croutons.

For this recipe, you may use store-bought cornbread from a grocery store commonly found in the bakery department or use leftover cornbread. Cut cornbread into ½ inch – ¾ inch cubes and bake in toaster oven or oven for 10 minutes at 400°F or until brown.

SWEET POTATOES

I remember the first time I tasted a yam I loved (I later learned it was, in fact, a sweet potato, but I digress). I was at my Aunt Daisy's home after school. Occasionally, I would visit her and my Uncle Floyd, and she would feed me dinner. My Aunt Daisy was never one to mince words. She always had a way of explaining life lessons to make me suddenly see things differently.

The same can be said for what she taught me about food. It was at her home that I was reintroduced to foods that I had previously sworn off. I was never a huge fan of nuts in my desserts, but I cherished her Italian cream cake. I detested meatloaf because of its mushy mix of ground meats and eggs, squishy tomatoes, and stale bread-ends. But when my Aunt Daisy made her meatloaf, suddenly it became a childhood favorite. Likewise, I loathed sweet potatoes. To be honest, I don't recall if I'd tasted them before, but I had made up my mind that I hated them. But all it took was for my Aunt Daisy to change my mind. I remember they looked like orange sausage patties. I later learned that the sweet potatoes were the only part of the meal that hadn't been made from scratch; Aunt Daisy had simply taken them out of a package and heated them in the oven and slathered with rich butter. But it didn't matter. That afternoon, I learned one of the most important life lessons: try everything at least once. You just might like it.

From my initial stance of hatred, I grew to love every form of sweet potatoes: roasted, mashed, in a casserole, fried, savory, or served sweet in a pie. Mistakenly referred to as a yam, the two root vegetables are often used interchangeably, though they are (surprisingly) not even related.

"[On the slave ship to America, we] had nothing to eat but yams, which were thrown amongst us at random–and of those, we had scarcely enough to support life," an enslaved African told a free black in Charleston. "More than a third of us died on the passage, and when we arrived at Charleston, I was not able to stand."

Yep. You read that right folks. Sweet potatoes and yams are NOT IN THE SAME FAMILY. Although yams and sweet potatoes have similar appearances and are both flowering plants with edible tubers underground, there's a lengthy scientific explanation that basically boils down (pun intended) to how yams are monocots (plants with one embryonic seed leaf), and sweet potatoes are dicots (plants with two embryonic seed leaves).

The native yams from Africa were quite starchy and dry, very different from those cultivated and used in desserts today. In West Africa, before the slave trade, Africans roasted yams over an open fire. They would peel back the charred skin to expose the creamy white flesh. Other times, they boiled and mashed yams into porridge.

Sweet potatoes, on the other hand, are known for their unmistakable orange flesh, smooth skin, and tapered ends. So, if the two are so drastically different, how did they become synonymous? Simple. Like with most of the other recipes mentioned in this book, slaves resourcefully adapted what was available to them in their new unfamiliar land to compensate for dishes from their homeland. In other words, slaves began preparing sweet potatoes to replace the common yam because they were the closest, most prevalent root vegetable they could find. However, West Africans were put off by the unexpected sweetness. Still, they used the potatoes and eventually came to love them because they were plentiful and easily accessible. British immigrants brought with them their specialty of making pumpkin pies for dessert. Pumpkins were not as common in the South as they were up North, so Southerners used their next best commodity, sweet potatoes.

Slaves who baked sweet potato pies for their white owners began making the dessert as a treat for their own families to enjoy on special occasions when they were given extra flour, sugar, and sweet potatoes. After 400 years, sweet potato pies are classic sweet treats that continue to be served during holidays and Sunday afternoons.

CANDIED BOURBON WHIPPED SWEET POTATOES

Estimated Time: 45 minutes
Servings: 6

Ingredients–

6 LARGE SWEET POTATOES, PEELED AND CUT INTO MEDIUM SIZE CHUNKS

1/3 CUP UNSALTED BUTTER

1/2 CUP HALF AND HALF, MILK, OR HEAVY CREAM

2 CUPS BROWN SUGAR

1 TABLESPOON ORANGE JUICE

1 TABLESPOON ORANGE ZEST

2 TABLESPOONS BOURBON (USE VANILLA OR OTHER FLAVORING IF YOU PREFER NO ALCOHOL)

1/4 TEASPOON SEA SALT

Gourmet taste buds? Consider these optional toppings:

- thick-cut bacon cooked and chopped
- cooked sage leaves
- brown butter
- prosciutto cooked and chopped

---

1. Add the potato chunks to a large pot and cover with cold water. Bring the potatoes to a boil and cook for about 30 minutes until they are fork tender.
2. While potatoes are cooking, begin candied bourbon "sauce". In a separate pot over medium-low heat, add the following: butter, cream, sugar, orange juice, and zest. Heat until mixture is thoroughly combined. It should be bubbly and have a velvety smooth texture similar to caramel. Add bourbon to finish and remove from heat. Transfer into serving dish and cover to keep warm until potatoes are ready to serve.
3. When the potatoes are finished cooking, drain them and add them back to the pot. Mash them with a fork or potato masher. (If you have a potato ricer, I'd highly recommend using it to give potatoes a light and creamy texture.)
4. After the potatoes are mashed, use a whisk or electric hand mixer to whip them.
5. Once whipped, add in 1/3 cup of the reserved candied-bourbon sauce. Whip the potatoes again until everything is combined. Taste the potatoes and add the salt, seasoning more or less, if desired.
6. Serve whipped potatoes immediately with remaining sauce. Add optional suggested toppings right åbefore serving.

EASY 3 INGREDIENT SWEET POTATO GNOCCHI

Estimated Time: 30 minutes

Servings: 4-5

Ingredients–

2 LARGE SWEET POTATOES

2 ½ CUPS OF ALL-PURPOSE FLOUR (1/2 CUP RESERVED FOR FLOURING)

2 TEASPOONS OF SALT

To make the gnocchi:

1. Preheat the oven to 400°F. Poke a few holes in the sweet potatoes so steam can escape while baking. Bake the sweet potatoes for 40-50 minutes or until tender. You'll know they're done when a fork can be pressed in easily. Set aside until cool enough for you to handle them easily (about 10 minutes).
2. Combine the salt and 2 cups of the flour. Flour a work surface and pour your flour mixture onto the surface. Make a well in middle of flour.
3. Once the sweet potatoes are cool enough to handle, remove the skin and place them, one at a time, into the potato ricer. Rice both potatoes right on top of the flour (see picture to the right).
4. Once all the potatoes have been riced, flour your hands and begin working the sweet potato into the flour. Continue to mix until it's thoroughly combined into pasta dough.
5. Once fully combined, roll the pasta dough into a ball and cut it into eight even pieces. Roll each piece into a long log or rope that's about 1 inch thick.
6. Next, cut dough into 1-inch pieces. Very carefully toss each piece into flour to ensure that it's dry and not sticky at any edges. Continue until you've cut out pieces from all of the dough.
7. Optional: Use a gnocchi board or fork to press grooves into each piece of gnocchi.
8. You may cook the gnocchi right away or store the gnocchi (in the refrigerator for up to 3 days or in the freezer for a few weeks).

To cook the gnocchi:

9. Salt your water and bring to a boil. Add gnocchi and let cook for roughly 2 minutes. Once the gnocchi floats to the surface of the water, let it boil for 20-30 more seconds and then remove it from the water using a slotted spoon.

Gourmet taste buds? Toss in your favorite sauce (I like to toss mine in a bit of brown butter and fresh herbs like rosemary or thyme). To really lift the flavor profile of the dish, I often love to cook a bit of prosciutto or other salty pork until crispy and then add sage or rosemary.

OKRA

Serving stewed meats and vegetables such as okra together are commonly referred to as "gumbo" in the southern United States region, and very similar dishes are traditionally served in Africa. Although nowadays okra is popularly seen as a generically "Southern" side dish, it is yet another food derived from West Africa. Although the slave trade stripped Africans of their identities and rights, slaves preserved their recipes and methods from their homeland. In fact, the word "gumbo" originates from the Bantu word for okra, ki ngombo. The Senegalese often used okra when cooking to thicken stews and soups. This practice was later adopted to New Orleans-style cooking.

Another recipe that was the precursor to the famous gumbo is the traditional West African okra stew called okro soup. Its list of ingredients reads similar to that of gumbo: fresh okra, shrimp or shellfish, and a hearty, rich sauce.

At the tender age of eight, I was known around my neighborhood as quite the lemonade and cookie "tycoon". Our front yard was enormous, and I was an only child so I spent many days outdoors mulling around attempting to keep myself occupied. Well, one day I asked my mother if she would help me sell lemonade and cookies outside because I thought it looked "fun" when I saw children on tv do it. At any rate my mother graciously allowed me to use her 1977 AMC Gremlin as the "quaint" store front for my budding entrepreneurial spirit. It was a vibrant orange tiny car with two black racing stripes along the sides. I would sit crouched in the trunk and when I saw the mailman (one of about five people who brought my annual revenue to a whopping $12, give or take, for the entire summer) I would carefully fling open the hatchback and proudly exclaim, "I have cookies and lemonade for sale!" Thinking back, I probably looked like a crazed child escaping from the gapes of an overgrown jack-o-lantern in the sweltering Southern heat. Still not sure why I didn't just let them read the signs vs. me flailing around hysterically pleading for innocent bystanders to drink my lemonade. I think deep down I always knew that selling items out of a mobile unit was a brilliant idea. Okay, so I never said it was an original idea...but brilliant nonetheless.

At some point between the late '80s and early '90s, home delivery services become popular. Before Amazon or UberEats food delivery, we had the Schwan's Food Truck, and, in Sherman, a man just known as "The Wig Man." I have no idea what his name was because that was all my grandmother ever called him. The Wig Man delivered, well, wigs in the back of a white storage truck. He'd pull right up to Bigmama's front yard and extend his step ladder down from his oasis of ash blondes,

chestnuts, gingers, and raven-haired wig heads. Back in the day, I imagine my grandmother felt for The Wig Man (or, at least, for his wigs) what I felt for my ninth-grade crush, Brett Atchison. When I saw Brett, my heart would race, and I would imagine us walking – no skipping - hand in hand down the high school corridor towards our shared locker. (FYI, shared lockers in high school are the equivalent of shacking as an adult.)

Just when we thought it couldn't get any better, The Wig Man starts operating another truck on different days of the week, selling fresh vegetables like an ice cream truck for old folks. Now on Saturdays Bigmama could buy a new wig for church and on Tuesdays she could buy fresh okra. The second truck had rows and rows of greens, sweet potatoes, cabbage heads, and okra. My grandmother prepared all these frequently, but what I remember most is her okra. I couldn't appreciate it then. Like many others, I was turned off by its sliminess, which is ironically why the Africans used it most, since its sugar residues thicken when added to soup and stew. Bigmama would prepare her okra and stewed tomatoes almost daily and place them on her stove.

When I would walk into the kitchen, I'd see the food sitting in Pyrex dishes along with her other favorites. Today I eat okra in my gumbo and other dishes, and recently I've begun buying crispy okra from Trader Joe's as a snack. It's delicious!

I wanted to recreate okra into something I could serve as a side dish to someone who didn't care for the slimy center. I discovered that baking them quickly at high heat drastically reduces the gooeyness and makes for a beautiful presentation with its charred look. It tastes sensational when served alongside a spectacular main course.

In 2015, after being laid off from a job I'd had for 10 years, I leveraged my talent for cooking into a career. Swanky underground supper clubs and clothing pop-up shops were becoming popular in large cities like New York. The non-committal nature of a pop-up piqued my interest, so I started my own pop-up restaurant inspired by my favorite meal, brunch, turning traditional foods into easy-to-eat, handheld favorites. Items like my best-selling chicken and waffle sandwich with peach bacon jam and fresh arugula, the popular stuffed shrimp and grit fritters with an accompanying creamy remoulade dipping sauce, and my creamy spin on collard greens made my small outdoor eatery an easy sell at the local downtown farmers market.

Like the other brunch items, the following okra recipe is a twist on a Southern classic. I love okra, but it's nice to challenge yourself by taking an already-delicious item and switching it up. Roasting the okra offers crispy burnt ends without a bitter taste, and the chili and lime zest is just the right subtle flavor to remind me of the Southwest.

Chili Lime Okra

Estimated Time: 25 minutes
Servings: 5

Ingredients–

1 POUND FRESH OKRA

1 TABLESPOON OLIVE OIL

1 TABLESPOON SEA SALT

1 LIME, ZESTED AND JUICED

CHILI PEPPER FLAKES

1. Preheat oven to 425 °F.
2. Toss fresh okra with olive oil in a bowl.
3. Add 1 tablespoon sea salt and 3 teaspoons chili pepper flakes to okra.
4. Zest one lime and pour juice over okra.
5. Transfer okra to baking sheet and place in oven 25-30 minutes until okra is charred and roasted.

CHICKEN

In addition to foods like okra and yams, enslaved Africans brought their cooking techniques too. As with many culinary traditions, enslaved Africans have been largely erased from the barbeque. Even the word barbecue has roots in West Africa among the Hausa, who used the term "babbake" to describe a complex of words referring to grilling, toasting, building a large fire, singeing hair or feathers and cooking food over a long period of time over an extravagant fire. The process would begin days in advance, and because it was so time-consuming, they began doing this practice only during celebratory occasions (along with the sorrel drink). After the Africans were enslaved in the States, they gained influence from the Spanish (barbacoa) and Native Americans when barbecuing.

But because their diet mostly consisted of pork (bad cuts) and corn, they would incorporate what they learned in Africa to cover the taste, spicy marinades of hot pepper and vinegar sometimes served with a rich tomato-based sauce on the side. If that sounds familiar, it's because although barbecue is prepared differently regionally, North Carolina's sauce is still vinegar-based and much of Texas' barbecue is tomato or ketchup-based.

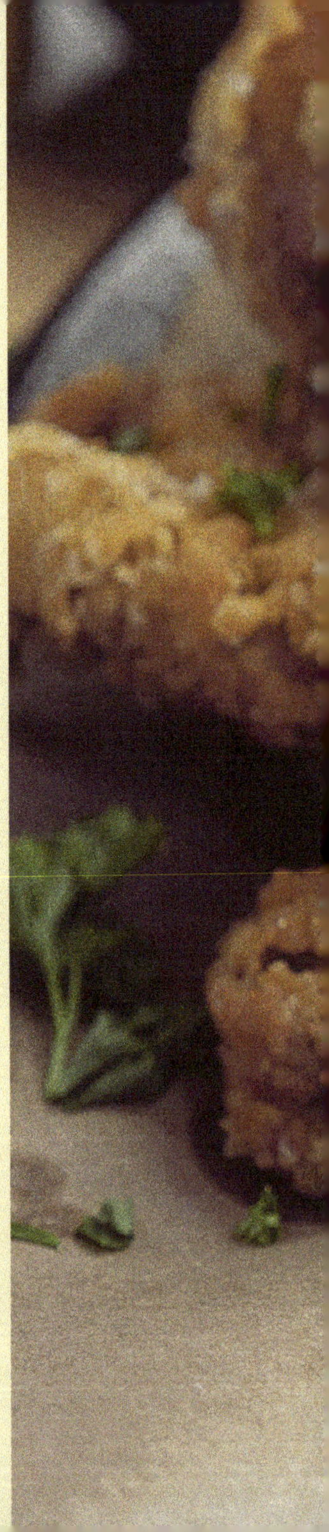

Today fried chicken is a staple in many households (both Northern and Southern), but especially those in the Black community. How did this come to be? Southern states often had the agriculture and the climate to sustain raising chickens. Even though chickens originated in Asia, they became standard food in North and West Africa. However, in North America, foods were reserved for the plantation owners, and slaves were left to make do with scraps the owners discarded. Chickens and other farm animals were prepared for the "big house," and Africans were forbidden from eating this meat. Instead, slaves were provided with rations that often included a heavy diet of grains and vegetables. Chicken most likely eventually found its way into slave quarters through the house slaves, who had access and knowledge of cooking ingredients.

For as long as I can remember chicken has always held a special place in my heart. Like a distant cousin, it's been a constant in our homes for Sunday after-church dinners, seasonal holidays, funeral repasses, or regular Wednesday afternoons. In fact, there are few places in the South where you could not find this iconic recipe on the menu. As a high-schooler, it was not uncommon to see a cloud of smoke billowing up from my childhood home as the school bus dropped me off. Be it a thunderous downpour or sweltering Texas heat, there was a strong chance that my mother was probably making chicken… again. She'd eat it grilled, stuffed, fried, sautéed or smothered; she had no loyalty to any method of preparation. Despite the almost overkill frequency, I never tired of poultry - that is, until I moved to Houston after high school. I had to ride the Greyhound back to my hometown of Sherman.

After sitting idly for three hours or so, the bus rolled into its rest stop midway through. As the newest passengers found their seats, fate would have it that my neighbor approached me. An

During the Jim Crow era, many Black families still practiced the tradition of frying chicken to pack with them for long train or car rides. They packed their dinners not only for convenience, but out of necessity, due to discrimination laws that prevented non-Whites from patronizing some restaurants, hotels, rest stops, and gas stations. As a response to this problem, in 1936 a mailman named Hugo Green began publishing an annual guide for African-American road-trippers, who were fearful of being beaten, arrested, or killed. The Negro Motorist Green Book encouraged Black travelers to hit the road without as much hesitation.

older man with tattered clothes and a ruddy face plopped down beside me with two brown paper bags in tow. One bag was greasy and reeked of old chicken. The second bag…well, I'm sure you can guess what that contained.

Within seconds of leaving our stop, he began to rip into his greasy bag and eat the cold chicken. As I peered at him under the guise of reading a book, he tore into the flesh before taking a swig of his other bag. Eat. Then swig. This went on for about 30 minutes until the driver made an unexpected stop to kick him off the bus.

Despite that harrowing encounter, it's safe to say that when I started cooking for myself, chicken was the furthest thing from my budding food repertoire. Then I discovered Popeye's fried chicken. I know it's cliché, but if I could get away with eating that stuff 75% of the week,

I probably would. I'm a sucker for dark meat – legs and thighs are my favorites. As for chicken breasts, I always found white meat too dry to be pleasurable. When I met my boyfriend, one of the first dishes he prepared for me was chicken. His method of preparation is simple but yields some of the best-tasting chicken I've ever eaten.

Just like with Popeyes, if I had a choice, I'd eat his chicken much more often. This recipe combines two things I love: the smokiness of grilled meat over hot coals and the crunchy yet flaky skin. It uses a simple buttermilk marinade with one small addition of an easy to find pantry ingredient.

For another little twist on this classic, I've added potato starch to my dry mix ingredients, inspired by the crunchier chicken I encountered on a trip abroad to my father's homeland of Japan. If you prefer a flakier crust, feel free to omit.

SMOKED FRIED CHICKEN

Estimated Time: 1 day prep + 45 minutes
Servings: 5

Ingredients–

4LBS OF CHICKEN (SKIN ON-BONE IN) CUT INTO PIECES

6 CUPS LARD/PEANUT OIL OR CANOLA OIL (FOR FRYING)

Brine:

3 CUPS BUTTERMILK

2 TEASPOONS GOOD QUALITY LIQUID SMOKE

3 GARLIC CLOVES, MINCED

2 SPRIGS FRESH ROSEMARY

2 TABLESPOONS SEA SALT

1 TABLESPOON WHITE PEPPER

1 TABLESPOON, HOT SAUCE (OPTIONAL)

Breading:

2 TABLESPOONS CAYENNE PEPPER

1 TEASPOON ONION POWDER

1 TEASPOON GARLIC POWDER

2 TEASPOONS SMOKED PAPRIKA

1 CUP POTATO STARCH, 2 ½ CUPS ALL-PURPOSE FLOUR

reserve about 25% of spices to add to chicken after removing from skillet

1. Mix brine ingredients and add chicken. Brine overnight or minimum three hours.
2. Remove chicken from refrigerator and let container sit 30 minutes or until room temperature. *Never put cold meat into hot grease. This will cause the meat to contract, making it tougher.*
3. Remove chicken from marinade and heat oil until 400°F.
4. Combine spices (making sure you reserve at least 3 tablespoons to season chicken after frying) and starch/flour in a large bowl.
5. Transfer wet chicken into dry ingredients and shake or pat until well-coated.
6. Repeat steps to double coat alternating brine and breading.
7. If you don't own a cooking thermometer, there are alternative methods of checking oil temperature.

   Here are two that I use. Once you see small bubbles just below the surface of the oil, near the bottom of the skillet, it has reached the correct temperature. You may also test the oil by placing the end of a wooden spoon directly into hot oil. If you see tiny bubbles surround th wooden handle the oil is hot enough to begin cooking. ***
8. Slowly add chicken pieces into skillet. (Make sure you don't overcrowd the pan.) Cover and check after 7-8 minutes or when chicken is golden brown. Turn chicken pieces and cover again for additional 7-8 minutes until desired golden color.
9. After removing chicken from oil, place on wire rack set over baking sheet to drain excess oil. Season with remaining seasoning mixture to your preference while hot.

SPATCHCOCKED PRESERVED LEMON ROAST CHICKEN WITH COLLARD GREEN PESTO

Spatchcocking is a cooking technique that involves splitting, then flattening chicken to produce an evenly roasted chicken with perfectly crisp skin and juicy flesh. In Northern Africa, chicken tagine is served with preserved lemons, olives and an herbaceous mix of cilantro and parsley. Here, I've kept the flavors of Morocco with the often paired yet contrasting flavors of sweet preserved lemons and briny olives. The chicken is balanced by a classic Southern staple of collard greens made in a pesto form.

Estimated Time: 40 minutes (Chicken roasts 25-30 minutes total)

Servings: 4

Ingredients:

1 WHOLE CHICKEN (SKIN-ON, SPATCH-COCKED)

1 12-OUNCE JAR PRESERVED LEMONS (RESERVE 4-5 TABLESPOONS JUICE)

4 GARLIC CLOVES, CRUSHED

10 PITTED OLIVES

4 TABLESPOONS BUTTER (UNSALTED)

1 TABLESPOON OLIVE OIL

7-8 TABLESPOONS COLLARD GREEN PESTO

SALT, BLACK PEPPER, FRESH HERBS: THYME, ROSEMARY (4-5 SPRIGS EACH)

1. Preheat oven to 500 degrees.
2. Allow chicken to sit at room temperature 30 minutes before seasoning with salt, pepper and fresh herbs. Don't forget to season all sides of chicken.
3. Liberally add 4-5 tablespoons collard green pesto to chicken massaging into both sides. Rub underneath skin if you have remaining pesto leftover.
4. Cover chicken with preserved lemon slices and pour 4-5 tablespoons preserved lemon juice over chicken.
5. Add olive oil to cast iron skillet to coat bottom of pan, then toss in crushed garlic.
6. Place breast side up in skillet. Roast 15 minutes. Remove from oven and add whole olives and pats of butter over chicken. Return to oven.
7. After 5 or 10 additional minutes, the chicken should be uniform in color. The skin will appear shiny and a medium brown hue. The bright green pesto has baked in so you will add more on top now for presentation purposes.
8. Finish with remaining 3 tablespoons pesto spooned lightly over top of chicken.
9. Roast chicken until juices run clear when pierced between breast and leg (an instant-read thermometer should read 165 degrees when inserted in thickest part of a thigh, avoiding bone).

COLLARD GREEN PESTO

This collard green pesto is rich and vibrant! Here it is paired with the Moroccan-inspired chicken dish but I often use it in many other dishes as well. Further into this book you'll find my recipe for spiced lamb and this can be used instead of the mint gremolata. I have also added this pesto in pasta, with beef skirt steak, or as a sandwich condiment. My partner has a nut allergy so I often find ways to replace recipes calling for nuts (when possible). The use of pumpkin seeds is not only healthy but allergen-free!

Makes about 1 ½ cups and can be covered and refrigerated up to 10 days.

Ingredients:

1 BUNCH/12-14 LEAVES COLLARDS, STEMMED AND DERIBBED

2 GARLIC CLOVES

½ TEASPOON KOSHER SALT

1 CUP OLIVE OIL

½ CUP PUMPKIN SEEDS, SHELLED AND SALTED

1 CUP PARMESAN CHEESE

Africans were accustomed to eating many vegetables and legumes. In Africa, their diet centered around stews served over a starchy base such as fufu, a mixture of boiled yams and cassava. These stews are echoed in Cajon, Creole, and Louisiana-style cooking, which often feature chicken or seafood with a sauce over a bed of rice. These meals are strikingly similar to a West African dish called okru.

TSIRE-SPICED LAMB CHOPS & MINT GREMOLATA

Another common protein cooked in parts of Africa is lamb. It is roasted, seared or grilled to develop the flavors and mixed with herbs and aromatic spices like a Tsire-blend that is used regularly as a coating for kebabs in West Africa. In Northern Africa, for example, thicker cuts of lamb are also stirred into soups and stews, marinating in rich red bases with red peppers or fiery scotch bonnet peppers. Lamb is also served with various herbed sauces to help cut the sometimes "gamey" taste diners reference. Mint pairs exceptionally well with this protein, so I created a mint-based gremolata, or a fresh citrus and herb-based condiment (like pesto without oil) that originated in Italy, to top this succulent dish.

MINT GREMOLATA

Ingredients:

1 TABLESPOON GRATED LEMON ZEST,

2 LEMONS

2 TABLESPOONS MINT, MINCED

1 TABLESPOON GREENS (I USE COLL

ARDS OR PARSLEY)

2 TEASPOONS MINCED GARLIC

3 TABLESPOONS PARMESAN CHEESE

2 TABLESPOONS PINE NUTS, TOASTED

(You may find pre-made Tsire spice blends online or in some ethnic grocery stores or aisles)

Estimated Time: 45 minutes
Servings: 4-6

*Mix all ingredients in a small dish. Cover and set aside to allow flavors to meld – or blend- together beautifully.

TSIRE SPICED LAMB CHOPS

Ingredients:

2 POUNDS LAMB CHOPS

4 SPRIGS ROSEMARY, FRESH

1 TABLESPOON TSIRE SPICE, MAY SUBSTITUTE ANY SPICE BLEND YOU PREFER

4 TEASPOONS SEA SALT

2 TEASPOONS BLACK PEPPER

4 GARLIC CLOVES, MINCED

6 TABLESPOONS OLIVE OIL, DIVIDED 4 TABLESPOONS FOR MARINADE MIX

2 TABLESPOONS BUTTER, CUBED (OPTIONAL)

---

1. Place lamb in a zip-top bag and add 4 tablespoons oil, 2 teaspoons salt, pepper, rosemary, and garlic. Set aside and marinate 30 minutes.
2. Allow lamb to come to room temperature before cooking and pat dry with paper towel to remove excess moisture (this is so that you'll get a better crust).
3. Preheat cast iron skillet over medium-high heat and preheat oven to 400 degrees.
4. Add just enough oil to lightly cover bottom of skillet.
5. Place lamb chops in skillet and quickly sear 1 to 2 minutes per side just to get a nice brown crust.
6. Quickly move pan to oven and roast 3-4 minutes.
7. Remove from oven and use tongs to place on cutting board to rest five minutes.
8. Optional) Place butter on immediately after removing from pan while resting.
9. Serve with gremolata as condiment.

I routinely listen to food-science podcasts, and one of them is called "Gastropod," hosted by Cynthia Graber and Nicola Twilley. In one episode they talked about the discovery of bread. By now it may not surprise you to know that the very first bread was created in Africa about 9,000 years ago! It was most likely unleavened round flat loaves of crushed wheat. Since yeast had not yet been discovered, the loaf must have been a far cry from the soft, fluffy buttermilk biscuits eaten in much of the South. Instead, it was a spongy flatbread, like the Injera bread still eaten by Northern Africans and Ethiopians today. Savory biscuits are eaten in the American South are commonly made with baking soda or baking powder as active chemical leavening agents instead of yeast.

The word "biscuit" is derived from the latin words for "twice baked". Very similar to Italy's cookie served with coffee – biscotti, which is a twice baked treat. Savory biscuits eaten in the American South today are commonly made with baking soda or baking powder as active chemical leavening agents instead of yeast. In the pre-Civil War south cornbread was by far the most popularly eaten bread. This is because of the mills that were prevalent in the Antebellum South. Many of them were only able to process corn properly, not the wheat in the flour used for baking biscuits. The only people able to have flour mailed to them were wealthiest people who could afford this luxury. For the rest, poor white settlers, indentured servants and slaves, there were various types of biscuits in the growing American lexicon. These are three of the most common.

- Cathead biscuits : Very similar to the biscuits commonly prepared today. Were typically hand-formed or drop biscuits, few ingredients used, easy to prepare, and it was given the name "cathead" because of its size resembling a feline's head.

- Sweet potato biscuits – As mentioned, because flour was one of the ingredients that was very hard to acquire, it was not always available. Sweet potatoes were used as a substitute for flour. You're not likely to find many recipes for this biscuit today that swap out flour completely, but this is how it was originally meant to be prepared – as a substitute.

- Beaten biscuits – The durable biscuit was made to withstand long trips. Imagine traveling many miles on foot and retrieving this thick cookie-like textured biscuit out of your nap satchel to eat after working all day in the hot fields.

Surprisingly, the biscuits most of us know and love today (soft, fluffy, layered) was introduced to our Northern neighbors fairly recently by none other than Kentucky Fried Chicken in 1952. In this year the up and coming mega-fried food producer had just opened a restaurant in Utah. Thus, beginning the world-wide love affair with the biscuit.

To make this the perfect quintessential "classic" Southern biscuit recipe simply omit the cheese and chives. These are absolutely divine served fresh out of the oven with a bit of good quality salted European butter and raspberry hibiscus jam slathered inside.

CHEDDAR AND GREEN ONION BUTTERMILK BISCUITS

This recipe calls for much more baking powder than most recipes I was accustomed to seeing, but the payoff was sensational! I'm not typically the baker in my family. That honor goes to my sister Sarah, however these are the ONLY biscuit recipe I've ever been successful at making. So simple and they rise very high so make sure yours are cooked thoroughly in the center. When baked perfectly your biscuits will be so tender and soft on the inside. Why do I recommend using European-style butter if you can? The butter fat is much higher which means you will have softer texture and a faster melt and the flavor more pronounced.

Ingredients-

2 ½ CUPS PASTRY FLOUR OR ALL-PURPOSE FLOUR (PLUS 2 TABLESPOONS FOR DUSTING)

2 TABLESPOONS BAKING POWDER

1 TEASPOON SALT

1 TEASPOON SUGAR

8 TABLESPOONS UNSALTED BUTTER (FROZEN AND CUBED)

1 CUP BUTTERMILK (PLACE IN FREEZER 15 MINUTES BEFORE STARTING RECIPE)

1 CUP SHARP CHEDDAR, SHREDDED

1/2 CUP OR FISTFUL OF GREEN ONIONS, CHOPPED

Estimated Time: 30 minutes
Servings: 1 dozen

1. Preheat your oven to 425 degrees. Line baking sheet with parchment paper or a silicone baking mat.
2. Sift the flour, salt, baking powder, and sugar in a mixing bowl.
3. Work the cold butter into the flour mixture using your fingers, a fork, or a food processor. You'll be looking for a crumbly texture similar to breadcrumbs. If using a blender or food processor pulse 6-7 times.
4. Pour buttermilk slowly over the flour mixture. Quickly and gently mix for about 15 seconds, until you've made a consistent dough.
5. Fold in half of cheese and green onions being VERY careful not to overwork your dough, or it will be dense.
6. Place the dough on a lightly floured work surface. Pat it into a rough rectangle about 1" inch thick. Fold it into thirds like a letter and roll GENTLY with a floured rolling pin until the dough is an inch thick and fold in half. Roll gently until dough is about an inch thick.
7. Cut the dough into circles with a biscuit cutter for traditional round biscuits, or use a knife to cut square biscuits. Make sure your biscuit dough is touching! Note: I prefer to make square biscuits because they don't leave dough scraps behind.
8. Bake the biscuits for 10-13 minutes, until they're lightly browned. Remove them from the oven, and serve warm.
9. Brush with melted salted butter if desired.

***You may substitute any milk (heavy cream, milk, half and half, buttermilk) for this recipe. For better results, always use ice cold dairy ingredients and bowls when making biscuits.**

RATIONS

"Kenyere" in Igbo

"Those who are at one regarding food are at one in life."
—Malawian Proverb

Since the inception of chattel slavery in the United States, thousands of Africans were captured and taken to North America, South America, and the Caribbeans. Complex systems of punishment such as language, culture, food, and religion to further subdue the enslaved into a lifetime of captivity.

In Saltwater Slavery: A Middle Passage from Africa to American Diaspora, Stephanie E. Smallwood describes in detail how elaborate systems of punishment were used to break down Africans mentally, physically and emotionally; they were treated as commodities. (Stephanie Smallwood, Saltwater Slavery: A Middle Passage from Africa to American Diaspora (Cambridge: Harvard University Press, 2007), 34-35.) As they were sold off to different plantation owners in different regions, slaves were torn from their family and loved ones. With many of them now suffering from severed familial bonds, slaves faced an overwhelming sense of seclusion, which was further intensified by language barriers. West Africa had several distinct languages and cultures, and many slaves had added difficulties communicating due to an inability to locate others who spoke their same language on their plantation. Afraid and left with minimal methods to communicate, slaves were left with yet another challenge: their diet.

There are various forms of slavery, but in the context of this book we will refer to Chattel slavery, which is commonly associated with the American south. This type of slavery where human beings are considered to be property and are bought and sold as such. It is the kind of slavery that existed before the Civil War in the United States.

Perhaps for the first time in many of their lives, rations restricted food choice, but slaves could sometimes supplement meals with hunting, fishing, and gardening at night, after excruciating labor. West African agriculture incorporated many of the same crops as the South, such as rice (Robert L. Hall, "Africa and the American South: Culinary Connections," Southern Quarterly 44.2(2007), 20-21). Recipes included shrimp (along with the coastal regions), catfish, cornmeal, bacon fat, black-eyed peas, discarded animal parts, chitlins, and oxtails. Not only did this method of control give rise to the aforementioned dishes, but it also embraced simple and delicious foods like cucumbers, tomatoes and onions marinated in a bit of vinegar – a dish my grandmother made weekly.

Additionally, the Native American influence of incorporating corn into dishes played a significant role in the dietary habits of African-Americans. Although the rations provided to slaves were sometimes also commonly used...to feed cattle, they became the sustenance that would fuel generations to come.

The injustice of food rationing persisted beyond slavery into the 21st century in malicious and intentional ways. Governmental policies such as the 1937 U.S. Housing Act, backed by President Franklin Roosevelt, made it legal for home loans to be denied to anyone living in neighborhoods where Blacks resided. As a result, this discriminatory policy not only kept groups of people separated by race, but also restricted access to, and therefore consumption of, healthy foods in certain areas. Many grocery stores were not willing to build in areas where higher minority demographics occupied the homes. Also, during the 20th century, residential neighborhoods began to evolve, and traffic increased. In 1956 (ironically the same year the Supreme Court outlawed bus segregation), policymakers began construction of highways to encourage intrastate travel. These new roadways did more than promote travel between cities and states; they also restricted low-income areas, predominantly Black communities, from accessing work, retail spaces, and, most notably, supermarkets that were not built in their neighborhoods. Even today, many lower-income areas are food deserts, areas where affordable and nutritious food is difficult to acquire, particularly for those without access to vehicles.

To eradicate this challenge, many nonprofits and individuals are making great strides to reach out to the community and improve the lives of residents. National nonprofit American Heart

Association (AHA) and local nonprofits such as Dallas's Feed Oak Cliff are encouraging healthy eating habits while also advocating for healthy restaurants and grocery stores.

According to the U.S. Department of Agriculture, 25-30 million Americans live in food deserts. Outside of restricting dietary choices, food desert conditions have been proven to lead to many chronic other diseases such as heart disease and diabetes, two ailments that plague the African-American race at a much higher rate than others. Centers for Disease Control and Prevention, "Health Disparities Experienced by Black or African-Americans -- United States," writes the following statistics:

• Diabetes is 60% more common in black Americans than in white Americans. Blacks are up to 2.5 times more likely to suffer a limb amputation and up to 5.6 times more likely to suffer kidney disease than other people with diabetes.

• Blacks develop high blood pressure earlier in life -- and with much higher blood pressure levels -- than whites. Nearly 42% of black men and more than 45% of black women aged 20 and older have high blood pressure

Including vegan dishes in this book was a natural conclusion because of these rising statistics, but also because I try to practice eating plant-based meals as much as possible. I am a culinary instructor and also work full time for the American Heart Association. I read articles daily about the rising cholesterol and high blood pressure numbers of Americans, particularly those of us of African descent. However, it is also personal for me. Not only do I read these articles, but I have family members and friends whose health has been impacted in part by the foods they have eaten daily. Every month I log onto Facebook, and I am greeted by glib "RIP" posts from people who have lost classmates to strokes, heart attacks or they are living with diabetes. Personally, I have suffered from acid reflux constantly. Every day I am conscious of all these things, and yet tomorrow I will get up and continue to eat red meats and consume fatty cheeses. I look at my own aging body in the mirror and often wonder, "Am I next?"

This is not an attempt to scare anyone into healthy living. I am hopeful that you would consult your physician and make decisions by researching what is best for YOU. This is, however, meant to highlight the disparities in health among multicultural communities (the new legal rationing systems) and encourage healthier diets by introducing alternative dishes into your everyday cooking routine. You can certainly still enjoy the foods we've become accustomed to by way of rationing like low-country dishes that incorporate coastal favorites such as shrimp and grits or fried catfish in moderation. Perhaps try different methods of preparation– like my flavorful blackened catfish tacos (page 59).

VEGAN TEXAS-STYLE CHILI WITH CASHEW SOUR CREAM

Both the walnuts and corn are untraditional chili ingredients, but both add a great contrast in texture and flavor! The walnuts are a common meat replacement in vegan dishes, and the corn adds a nice touch of sweetness to complement the other flavors. If you have a nut allergy, simply omit the walnuts.

As for the vegan sour cream, it will probably not taste like sour cream when eaten alone; however, when you add it to dishes like this chili, it is exceptionally delicious and makes for a great dairy-free substitute!

Chili:

Ingredients–

2 TABLESPOONS OLIVE OIL

3-4 LARGE GARLIC CLOVES, MINCED

1 LARGE ONION OR 2 MEDIUM ONIONS, CHOPPED

3 – 4 TABLESPOONS CHILI SEASONING POWDER

1/4 TEASPOON BLACK PEPPER

2 TABLESPOONS DRIED ROSEMARY

1 ½ CUPS VEGETABLE BROTH OR A 12-OUNCE CAN OF BEER

2 CUPS CHOPPED BELL PEPPER, ANY COLOR

30 OZ. CAN DICED TOMATOES (I USE FIRE ROASTED)

15 OZ. CAN PETITE DICED TOMATOES

2 TABLESPOONS MAPLE SYRUP, AGAVE, HONEY OR BROWN SUGAR

2 TABLESPOONS AMINO ACID OR SOY SAUCE

1 TEASPOON SALT

1 TEASPOON LIQUID SMOKE

3-4 CUP WATER

2 TABLESPOONS LEMON JUICE

1/4 CUP UNCOOKED QUINOA

30 OZ. CANNED KIDNEY BEANS, DRAINED AND RINSED WELL

2 CUPS FRESH OR FROZEN CORN KERNELS

1 ½ CUP CRUSHED WALNUTS, IF DESIRED FOR EXTRA PROTEIN AND "MEATY" TEXTURE

Vegan Cashew Sour Cream:

Ingredients–

1 CUP RAW, UNSALTED CASHEWS

1/2 CUP WATER

2 ½ TABLESPOONS OF LEMON JUICE

1 ½ TABLESPOON APPLE CIDER VINEGAR

1/2 TEASPOON MAPLE SYRUP

1/2 TEASPOON SEA SALT

FRESH CILANTRO, AVOCADO OR VEGAN CHEESE SHREDS FOR TOPPING (OPTIONAL)

How to make chili:

1. Add the oil, garlic, and onion to a large pot. Sauté over medium heat for about 3 minutes.
2. Add the chili seasonings, black pepper, and any other seasonings. Add a few splashes of the beer/broth to deglaze the pan and simmer 3-4 minutes. Reduce the heat to medium-low and add more seasonings if they begin to burn off too quickly.
3. Stir in the bell pepper and the rest of the broth or beer. Simmer about 5-7 minutes.
4. Add the canned tomatoes, maple syrup, liquid amino or soy sauce, salt, liquid smoke, and water. Cover loosely and simmer for about 30 minutes, stirring occasionally.
5. Stir in the lemon juice, quinoa, black beans, walnuts (optional), and corn. Place lid on pot and simmer for about 50 minutes, stirring occasionally. Add 3-4 cups water for consistency, at your discretion.
6. Serve with vegan cashew sour cream to cut spiciness. On top, you may add the suggested toppings.

How to make the vegan sour cream:

7. Place cashews in a bowl or jar (I like using a wide-mouth quart mason jar) and cover with water. Let soak overnight (at least 8 hours).
8. Once soaking is finished, drain and rinse the cashews and place in the basin of a high-powered blender. Add in 1/2 cup of water, the lemon juice and zest, the apple cider vinegar, the maple syrup, and the salt. Blend these ingredients for about 3 minutes on high until very smooth.
9. Refrigerate for about an hour. The cream will thicken as it cools. Store in covered container in the fridge for up to 10 days

EASY BLACKENED CATFISH

Estimated Time: 10 minutes
Servings: 4

Ingredients–

4 CATFISH FILLETS

COOKING SPRAY

1 CUP BLACKENING SEASONING

1 ½ TABLESPOON COOKING OIL OR BUTTER

1 HEAVY PINCH SEA SALT

How to make blackened catfish:

1. Preheat dry cast iron skillet or grill pan.
2. Add 1 tablespoon cooking oil to skillet.
3. Place paper towel over fish and remove excess water. Pat until dry.
4. Brush remaining cooking oil over fish.
5. Cover each side liberally with blackened seasoning. (Make sure the entire fish is covered)
6. Lay fish on one side in skillet 2 minutes.
7. Carefully flip to opposite side 2-3 minutes to finish.
8. Remove fish from pan and season to taste with sea salt.
9. Plate with fresh squeezed lemon or lime.
10. Slice and serve in tacos.

Suggested taco ingredients:

½ MEDIUM RED ONION, CHOPPED

2/3 CUP CHOPPED CILANTRO

1 AVOCADO, SLICED

1 LIME OR LEMON, ZESTED AND JUICED

CHOPPED QUESO FRESCO OR COJITA CHEESE

½ CUP MEXICAN CREMA OR SOUR CREAM

BLACKENED CATFISH TACOS WITH CHARRED CORN

Charred Corn:

Ingredients–

3 CUPS FRESH OR FROZEN CORN KERNELS

PINCH SEA SALT

PINCH PEPPER

1. Sauté corn kernels in a preheated large cast-iron skillet on medium-high for 3 to 5 minutes, stirring constantly, until kernels are lightly charred.
2. Season with coarse sea salt and freshly ground pepper to taste. Serve immediately. (Can be made up to 1 day ahead, covered, and refrigerated.)

CUCUMBER, TOMATO AND, ONION SALAD

Combine cucumbers, tomatoes, and onion in a serving bowl. Add vinaigrette either immediately before serving or up to one hour in advance if slices are thin. (The thicker the sliced veggies the longer you may marinate in a covered dish in the refrigerator.)

Estimated Time: 15 minutes
Servings: 4

Ingredients–

3.LARGE CUCUMBERS, SLICED

1 PINT SMALL GRAPE TOMATOES OR CHAMPAGNE TOMATOES, SLICED LENGTHWISE

1 LARGE RED ONION, SLICED THINLY

1 TABLESPOON SEA SALT

2 TEASPOONS CRACKED BLACK PEPPER

2 TABLESPOONS VINAIGRETTE

Basic Vinaigrette
(can be refrigerated and stored up to 2 weeks)

¾ CUP OLIVE OIL (SUBSTITUTE CANOLA)

¼ WHITE WINE VINEGAR

2 TEASPOONS AGAVE NECTAR OR HONEY

½ PINCH OF SALT

¼ TEASPOON PEPPER

CHARRED CORN, AVOCADO, AND TOMATO SALAD

Estimated Time: 15 minutes
Servings: 6

Ingredients–

5 EARS OF CORN OR 1 BAG FROZEN CORN

½ RED ONION

1 LARGE OR 2 SMALL AVOCADOS

1 CUP GRAPE TOMATOES

1 LIME

½ TEASPOON OLIVE OIL

COARSE SEA SALT

1 TEASPOON MAPLE SYRUP, HONEY, OR NATURAL SWEETENER

1 CUP OF FRESH CILANTRO, CHOPPED

PROTEIN OF YOUR CHOICE (SHRIMP, GRILLED CHICKEN, OR FLANK STEAK), IF DESIRED

1. Preheat your broiler to medium-high.
2. Shuck your corn and remove the silks.
3. Cut the kernels from the cob with a knife and set them aside in a bowl. (If using frozen corn, simply remove from bag and follow the remaining steps.) Toss in olive oil to evenly coat. Transfer to a sheet pan (you can line with foil for easy cleanup) or large skillet and spread out in an even layer.
4. Broil the corn for 3 to 5 minutes, shaking the pan a few times, or until charred spots begin to appear. Remove pan from oven and allow corn to cool a few minutes.
5. While corn is cooling, prepare remaining salad ingredients.
6. Dice avocado and red onion and place in bowl.
7. Cut grape tomatoes in half and add to bowl.
8. Zest lime (making sure not to include the pith (white part), cut lime in half and add juice to salad.
9. Drizzle maple syrup or honey and ¾ tablespoon coarse sea salt into mixture.
10. Add corn to salad.
11. Chop cilantro and carefully mix all ingredients to evenly distribute.

If entertaining and serving to guests, add avocado last and immediately before serving. If desired, you may also add protein such as shrimp, grilled chicken or flank steak.

ROASTED PEPPER SAUCE

I created this sauce one day while cleaning out my refrigerator. What started as a menial task to get rid of leftovers has turned into one of my most treasured recipes. I use it as a base for pizzas, a topping for chicken or succulent shrimp dishes, and atop pasta in lieu of jarred sauces. It's quick and easy, and best of all you can control the ingredients. Coincidentally, it also inspired another recipe I adore, Autumn Harvest Sweet Potato Bisque.

Estimated time: 20-25 minutes
Servings: 4-6

Ingredients–

3 LARGE ROMA TOMATOES, QUARTERED

2 RED, ORANGE OR YELLOW BELL PEPPERS, ROUGH CHOPPED

½ YELLOW ONION, CHOPPED

4 LARGE GARLIC CLOVES, CRUSHED

3 SPRIGS FRESH ROSEMARY

1 ½ TABLESPOONS DRIED THYME

5 TABLESPOONS OLIVE OIL

1 TABLESPOON COARSE SEA SALT

CRACKED BLACK PEPPER (TO TASTE)

1 TEASPOON CHILI PEPPER FLAKES

½ CUP HEAVY CREAM

¼ CUP WHITE WINE, COOKING SHERRY WINE, OR VEGETABLE STOCK

½ TABLESPOON HONEY

1. Preheat oven to 425 degrees
2. Combine all vegetables and rosemary sprigs in shallow baking pan and lightly toss in 3 tablespoons olive oil
3. Add thyme to coat veggies before roasting
4. Roast 10-15 minutes until peppers, onions and tomatoes are softened and beginning to blister and char slightly. Remove from oven and set aside
5. Move contents of pan into high-powered blender
6. Add heavy cream and wine/liquid and blend until smooth
7. Add remaining 2 tablespoons olive oil, honey, sea salt, cracked black pepper and chili pepper flakes (optional)
8. Blend additional 30 seconds and serve warm

RED WINE BRAISED OXTAILS

1. Preheat oven to 225°F.
2. Heat olive oil over medium heat in large pot or dutch oven.
3. Coat oxtails with flour and generously season all sides of the oxtails with salt and pepper. Add seasoned oxtails to hot oil and give them a sear for 2-3 minutes on each side until oxtails are nice and browned on the outside.
4. Remove oxtails and set aside while sauce is prepared.
5. Return pot to burner and add onion and garlic. If the pan looks too dry, add another splash of olive oil. Sauté 2-3 minutes until onion has caramelized and appears translucent with a hint of brown.
6. Add salt and pepper to taste.
7. Add tomato paste and stir to combine.
8. Add red wine to deglaze. Make sure to scrape any browned bits off the bottom of the pan with a wooden spoon—this will blend with the oxtails while cooking to create a delicious sauce when the dish is complete!
9. Add bay leaves, beef stock and water to a pot and stir to combine. Bring the mixture up to a low simmer and then remove from heat.
10. Add oxtails back to the pot, nestling them in with the onions.
11. Cover and place in 225°F oven. Bake for 2 ½ hours, then uncover and add tomatoes.
12. Cover and cook additional 1 ½ hours.
13. Remove oxtails and let cool for 10-15 minutes.
14. If the broth looks too watery, you can bring it to a simmer over medium heat and cook it until reduces to a thicker consistency.
15. Garnish with a fresh, chopped parsley.

Estimated Time: 4.5 hours
Servings: 4

Ingredients–

6 LBS OXTAILS (OR SHORT RIBS)

4 TABLESPOONS OLIVE OIL

SALT AND PEPPER TO TASTE

1 LARGE YELLOW ONION, DICED

5 CLOVES GARLIC, MINCED

12 OZ RED AND YELLOW CHERRY TOMATOES (WHOLE)

2 TABLESPOONS TOMATO PASTE

2 CUPS PINOT NOIR (OR ANY OTHER RED WINE)

1 CUP BEEF STOCK

2/3 CUP WATER

2 BAY LEAVES

3 TABLESPOONS FLOUR

OPTIONAL: 3 TABLESPOONS CHOPPED FRESH PARSLEY FOR GARNISH

Hoecakes are near and dear to my heart. My grandmother, who partially raised me, would often make them, and they bring back fond memories. The name itself is the ultimate reflection of our people's ingenuity. Slaves received weekly rations, which would often include an allowance of pork, cornmeal, and lard, so they would mix the ground cornmeal with hot water and then, over an open fire, fry the simple gruel on the overturned backs of gardening hoes. Various forms of these hoecakes, also known in other regions as hot water cornbread or johnnycakes, are eaten not only in the United States, but also the Dominican Republic, the Bahamas, Bermuda, and other islands.

When my Bigmama would cook hoecakes, she never discussed the origins of the recipe. She only said that her father had made the meal for her when she was a child, and as she mixed her batter, I would watch anxiously as she poured her thick mixture into hot bubbling oil in a shiny black cast iron skillet.

I walked into a "Southern" restaurant nestled sweetly in the middle of a bustling gentrified neighborhood. It was owned by a popular (white) celebrity chef. I loved her "New Southern" approach to familiar, beloved soul food recipes. I was excited to see (and taste) her recreations. After studying the menu and questioning the servers about food pairings, we decided on a stack of hoecakes with a side of bacon and eggs and the crowd favorite, chicken and waffles with collard greens. While waiting for my food to come, I made small talk with the waitress as she wove in and out of our conversations to fill our water glasses.

"So…" I began curiously and half-joking. "do you know how this meal got its name?"

"Ummm. No," the cute blonde waitress giggled. "It's got a funny name, but they're kinda like pancakes but not as sweet."

The implication of promiscuity stunned me like a slap in the face. I wasn't sure if I was upset with the server for the ignorant comment or mad at the owner and chef for not educating staff. Hoecakes, along with many other items on their menu, had humble beginnings from a complex history. Perhaps the disdain I felt was with myself for patronizing an establishment that so obviously did not care enough about my people's traditions. Without a teachable moment, hungry guests would remain in the dark without recognizing the culture behind the food.

As the food began to arrive, I was further heartbroken that the dish was bland and unrecognizable. I felt hurt that the recipes I loved and respected had been watered down and that the art and history behind the food had been cast aside and forgotten... This is not to say other races cannot cook soul food favorites, but instead, I wanted people to appreciate how these dishes came to be. This fascinated me so much that, in one of my graduate courses, I wrote a term paper on the subject, which planted the seeds of this book...

SWEET CORN & OKRA HOECAKES

The recipe for my sweet corn and okra hoecakes is the easiest and most closely related to the original recipe. The simplicity lies in the fact that there never was a formal recipe, per say. Therefore, the ingredients below will be approximations.

Boil water and add to cornmeal until desired consistency. I prefer the mixture to be thicker than pancake batter. However thick you desire, the mixture should be just pourable, but thick enough that you'll need to use a spoon or spatula to help spread it out once it's in the pan. If it seems too thick, add anoter tablespoon or two of hot water. 2. After mixing these two ingredients, fold in fresh, chopped okra and sweet corn kernels shaved from the stalk (you may substitute fresh corn with frozen or drained can corn). I love playing with contrasting textures. I like the guessing game of whether I'll bite into something sweet, slightly salty or gritty. This makes the recipe more interesting and your dinner guests will appreciate it. Place a mound of cornmeal mixture (about 2 inches in diameter) in a hot skillet that has been lightly greased with any oil of your choosing. I like using canola oil because it has a high smoke point and I don't have to worry about it burning too quickly.

Other oils with high smoke points include corn, peanut, sunflower, and sesame. When the mounds have fried, place them on a paper towel to cool and let sit 5-6 minutes. Serve with a dollop of sour cream or Greek yogurt and add a hint of cayenne pepper for a kick and a nice pink hue. Hoecakes make an exceptional side dish, main dish, brunch, or appetizer.

Estimated Time: 20 minutes
Servings: Makes approximately 10-12 small hoecakes (2 inches in diameter)

Ingredients–

1 ½ cups water
1 cup fine ground cornmeal
½ fresh corn or frozen corn
5-6 okra chopped

CREATIVITY

“Nkà” in Igbo

“They ate our food, and forgot our names.”
—Tunisian Proverb

As I’ve referenced before, the African American culture is full of creativity and borrowing. From the resourcefulness required to turn subpar rations into bountiful meals that fed their families and communities to the unfamiliar foods they learned to prepare, African Americans persevered and prospered. They drew not just from their West

African roots and the demands of rations, but also from other origins, incorporating and tweaking. Some foods that we still eat today were derived Europe, the Caribbean, and South America. Potato salad, sweet potato pie, teacakes, fried green tomatoes, and even the king of the south macaroni and cheese, weren’t authentic Southern dishes until we stepped into the kitchens and used our ingenuity to recreate.

"When I was a lonely, scared and scarred eight-year-old, Mrs. Bertha Flowers, a lean, Black teacher invited me to her house and made teacakes. The aroma of the freshly baked cookies merged with the rich sound of her voice as she read to me.
" – *Maya Angelou*

The teacakes slaves baked were a direct response to the English tea cake. Typically made with fruit and yeast, English tea cake is toasted and then served with hot tea, not the sweet, syrupy sun tea we Southerners love. Slaves used what was readily available and made their own version to serve alongside other desserts with tea to impress guests after dinner.

As far back as I can remember, my grandmother was known across our small town as the unofficial "teacake connoisseur". I imagine she must have baked thousands of dozens throughout the years. How do you count all the birthday gifts, celebrations, and holidays when she lovingly prepared her pièce de résistance of every important meal of our lives? She never complained when people asked her to bake her famous dessert. On the contrary, she lived for those moments. If I close my eyes, I can still recall her buttery cookies with just the softest kiss of nutmeg. She baked them until they were the perfect hue – somewhere between maple sugar brown and caramel – before rushing to remove them for my cousin James, or sometimes my childhood friend

"Eat when the food is ready; speak when the time is right."
~Ethiopian Proverb

Adriane. (She knew I preferred mine a bit lighter, so she would take them out of the oven when they were about the color of the desert sands.) They somehow managed to be perfectly cooked on the outside, and soft and tender on the inside. They lingered on my tongue, and even before I knew what spices and seasonings were or how they enhanced our foods, I knew that something made them special. Something set her cookies apart from the ones other church folks tried to emulate. Hers was undoubtedly the best, and I am grateful for the legacy she left. I often think back to those days when I would watch her prepare her tea cakes and all the things we talked about. Some of the conversations she and I shared are slowly fading into sepia colored memories for me, and I hate I never asked her who taught her to share this gift with the world. She would pack them carefully in brown paper bags and deliver them to whoever the lucky recipients would be.

"The man who counts the bits of food he swallows is never satisfied."
~African Proverb

LAVENDER & BLUEBERRY TEA CAKES

Estimated Time: 30 minutes
Serving: 1 dozen

Ingredients–

½ CUP BUTTER FLAVOR CRISCO

½ CUP SUGAR

TEASPOONS BAKING POWDER

¼ TEASPOON BAKING SODA

¼ TEASPOON SALT

¼ CUP BUTTERMILK

1 ½ TEASPOON LAVENDER FLAVORING (FOR BAKING)

1/3 CUP FRESH OR FROZEN WHOLE BLUEBERRIES

1 EGG

TEASPOON VANILLA

1. Heat oven to 375 degrees.
2. Line baking sheet with parchment paper.
3. Beat sugar and Crisco together until light and fluffy.
4. Add in lavender flavoring and egg, then mix until well blended.
5. In a separate bowl, combine flour, baking powder, baking soda, and salt.
6. Alternate adding 1/3 of flour mixture into batter, along with buttermilk, stirring slowly, until all dry ingredients have been incorporated.
7. Roll dough ½ inch thick onto floured surface and cut with 2-inch round cookie cutter, biscui cutter or floured drinking glass rim.

BAKE AT 375 DEGREES FOR 10 MINUTES OR UNTIL COOKIE HAS REACHED DESIRED YOUR PREFERRED COLOR.

Now, let's get into this craziness about good ol' mac and cheese not being a food Black people invented. One would think from the way we proudly serve this plate at any and every gathering that we were responsible for bringing this cheesy exquisiteness over from the Motherland. Nope. Negative. Neanche per sogno! That's Italian, by the way, for "not even in your dreams."

This comfort food can trace its origins back to 13th-century Northern Italian roots. What began as a simple rustic food of pasta and parmesan spread across Europe and picked up subtle influences from various regions. For example, in France, cooking methods usually began with the mother of all French sauces, béchamel, a white sauce of butter, milk, and flour. With a bit of cheese, you've got the start of a killer mac and cheese today. In England during the 17th-century, casseroles and savory baked dishes were popular. You can, of course, see both influences in African-American version of macaroni and cheese. One key difference between African-American versions and, well, everyone else's, is that we typically don't serve our macaroni and cheese loose or wet. We bake the dish until it's bubbly, crisp and golden brown. The cheese forms a crust that is broken only by well-prepared knives and anxious spoons. Or at least most of "us" do. But, I'll let you in on a little secret that I rarely share with anyone. I prefer a more wet casserole. If I can cut my mac and cheese and it holds its shape, I don't want it. Ok, that admission felt good. I think I'd like to share another secret with you since we're so close now…are you ready? I make a killer vegan – yes, dairy-free- macaroni and cheese, and I'll fight you over it.

One person who helped usher in the wave of French-influenced cooking was none other than James Hemings, a Parisian trained chef and slave of President Thomas Jefferson. If the last name Hemings rings any bells, it's because he was the brother of Sally Hemings, the rumored mother to Jefferson's illegitimate children. James was Sally's older brother and left Jefferson's Monticello plantation, bound for Paris to be trained at one of the most prestigious culinary schools in Europe. France abolished slavery in 1794, so James earned a wage as Jefferson's chef while living there. However, upon returning to Monticello, he was considered a slave once again. Only a few Blacks were sent to France to be educated to teach others European techniques upon their

return. These Black cooks helped bring other French recipes such as meringues and crème brulees to the States.

After visiting Italy and tasting a dish similar to macaroni and cheese, Jefferson bought a pasta maker, returned to the United States, and had James create and serve macaroni and cheese at a White House dinner in 1802, which helped to popularize the dish.

Sadly, James committed suicide and never received the accolades he truly deserved while he was living. He would probably be proud to see all the different varieties of this classic favorite. Whether microwaveable or homemade with five-cheese blend and baked to a yellow-gold perfection, mac and cheese has come a long way from its humble beginnings.

So, the next time you're slouched over a stove stirring a golden pot of milk, butter, and cheese, think of James and how his revolutionary cooking brought a bit of Paris back to the United States.

Stanton, Lucia. "The Research File: From Plantation Fare to French Cuisine." Monticello Newsletter vol. 4, no. 2 (1993): 3

EASY BASIC PASTA RECIPE

I always tell people when I'm teaching my cooking classes, "Making homemade pasta is as easy as 1-2-3…literally." Remember these simple ingredients for any delicious pasta you may create. Once you're comfortable making this basic recipe, feel free to add herbs and/or various vegetables into your mixes. Also, feel free to play around with different shapes and sizes!

*Makes 1 pound of pasta

Ingredients–

1 TEASPOON SALT

2 CUPS FLOUR (SEMOLINA OR ALL-PURPOSE)

3 EGGS

1. Scoop flour onto clean flat surface (you may also use a bowl for the mixing step).
2. Make a well in center.
3. Add eggs and salt.
4. Mix thoroughly until dough ball forms. It will feel and look slightly rough, not too sticky and not too dry. If it becomes too loose, add flour to give it more body. If too dry, either add a pinch of olive oil or water.
5. This recipe is not like bread dough, which typically calls for as little handling as possible to ensure tenderness and fluffiness. Unlike bread, pasta loves to be mixed firmly! The longer you massage your dough, the more pliable it will be.
6. After ball is formed, wrap tightly in plastic wrap and let it sit out at least 30 minutes for your gluten to release and your dough to relax.
7. Unwrap ball of pasta dough. It should be soft, slightly shiny, and smooth.
8. Cut pasta into four pieces and begin to roll flat. Flour working area. Roll out each part of pasta thinly, on the floured surface, using a rolling pin. (Make sure to flour both the dough and roller to avoid any sticking.) The flatter you roll it, the better your finished product will be. In Italy, chefs roll their pasta until you can read a newspaper through it. If you can't get it quite that thin, as thin as possible is fine.
9. Decide what type of pasta you want. Once you've mastered beginner level pasta shapes, you can move on to more difficult sizes.

Popular beginner choices include:

- Pappardelle – wide flat noodle
- Fettucine – flat skinny noodle
- Ravioli – two sheets of thin pasta dough sealed together with filling inside

1. Bring a pot of salted water to a rapid boil then add pasta for 1-2 minutes . Fresh pasta cooks very fast! Remove it before it is cooked completely. This is known as "cooking al dente." After removing the pasta, it will continue to cook from the heat on its own.
2. Reserve approximately ½ cup to 1 cup of the pasta water. You can add this reserved water with fresh parmesan for a simple and creamy dish.

When I think of my dad I think of his kind, sweet, gentle demeanor. Other words that come to mind are: microwaves, "Banana Coat- Gate 1989", and spaghetti. Now that I think of it, I may owe a great deal of thanks to the man whom I most likely inherited most- if not all- of my eccentricities from. Peculiarities like, for example, my fear of microwaves. Never are you under any circumstances to stand directly in front of a microwave oven. I remember when I was a teenager I went to visit my dad and my then stepmother. I had innocently gone to place a plate in the microwave when as soon as I turned the dial I can still see him throwing his body in front of me (think WWII vet using his body as a human shield in front of a falling grenade to protect a fellow soldier) and carefully protecting me from ultra violet rays undetected by the naked eye.

In in the 8th grade all the "cool kids" were wearing popular starter jackets that were popularized by the bad boy rap group NWA. These coats were the urban youth's symbol of ghetto status and a way of weeding out the haves from the have-nots. I hoped, and I prayed desperately for months and when Christmas finally rolled around I saw a huge box wrapped in blue Santa Clause wrapping paper and tied neatly with a giant red bow. One glance at that box and I knew I had hit the outerwear jackpot! I envisioned myself wearing my new trophy to class and how the other girls would point and compliment my new thugged out street-style. I smiled to myself as I thought of all the pool party invites I would receive as soon as summer rolled around. I held my breath as I unwrapped the box and when I removed the lid and instead uncovered a giant puffy, neon

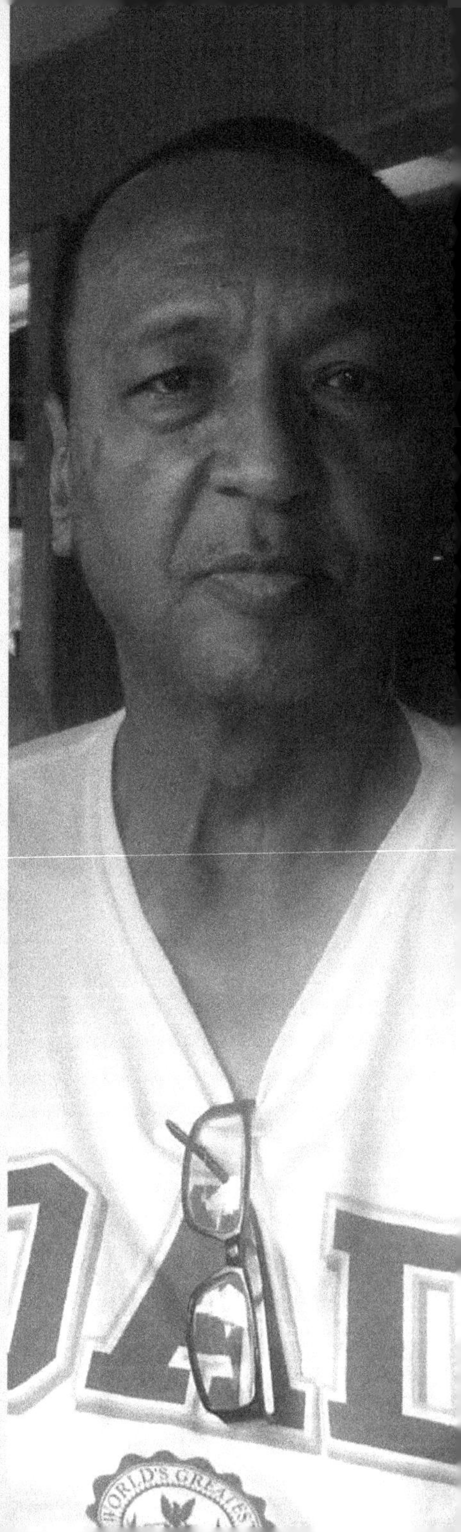

Me and Daddy, 2016

yellow coat with hot pink inner lining, I thought I would die from embarrassment. How could my father, a man who supposedly loved me so much, purchase such a thing? I guess my teenage language was lost in translation on my father, who in all honesty, heard me ask for a puffy LA Lakers starter jacket and translated this request to mean a giant neon yellow monstrosity that swallowed my tiny frame. I wore the coat to school when Christmas vacation was over, and I remember vividly racing out of class before any cute boy or cool girl could see me stuffing the neon yellow banana into my locker.

Sometimes I was successful, and other times the coat hung haphazardly out of my locker door stuffed between textbooks and packages of Hostess Twinkies. Although my mother is the more influential of the two, my dad is a good cook in his own rite. When I was younger I would watch him make his prized spaghetti that he was so proud of. It was delicious and had flavors I hadn't yet discovered. I found out later all he did was add Mrs. Dash seasoning to the meat and sauce, but at the time I thought it was so groundbreaking that he used something other than salt and pepper.

No, these recipes do not involve the use of Mrs. Dash – unless you decide so – but they are still prize-worthy in my opinion. Make at your own risk though, because it will require a microwave to reheat and my dad won't be there to save you.

VEGAN MAC & CHEESE WITH KALE

Yes, vegans can still enjoy the rich creamy cheddary goodness of cheese without actually inheriting the high cholesterol rates that can follow with eating these dishes we love.

Makes 5-6 servings

10.ounces cooked fettuccine

Ingredients-

noodles or macaroni

2 CUPS SAUTÉED KALE

VEGAN CHEESE SAUCE:

1 CUP PEELED/DICED YELLOW POTATOES (OR RUSSETS)

1 WHOLE CARROT, PEELED/DICED

1/3 CUP CHOPPED ONION

3/4 CUP WATER (PREFERABLY USE LIQUID FROM POT OF BOILED VEGGIES)

1/2 CUP RAW CASHEWS

1/4 CUP COCONUT MILK

2 ¼ TABLESPOONS NUTRITIONAL YEAST FLAKES

1 TABLESPOON LEMON JUICE

1 TEASPOON SALT (OR MORE TO TASTE)

1/4 TEASPOON GARLIC POWDER

1 PINCH CAYENNE PEPPER (OPTIONAL)

1 PINCH PAPRIKA

Instructions

1. Cook macaroni al dente, or cook until still slightly firm, according to package instructions (usually requires boiling for 6-8 minutes in salted water), drain, and set aside.
2. Add water, chopped potatoes, carrots, and onion and cook for about 10 minutes, or until water is boiling and vegetables are fork tender. When veggies are soft enough to blend, drain and reserve about ¾ cup to 1 cup of cooking water. Place all ingredients (including veggies) in a high-speed blender. Add 1/2 cup reserved water to test thickness of sauce. Be careful! If it is too thick add about ¼ more cup of reserved water. Be sure not to add too much water or you will risk making your sauce too watery.
3. Blend until smooth and creamy.
4. Pour sauce over your cooked macaroni noodles in a dish of your choice, taste for salt, add kale and serve immediately.
5. Or, if making a traditional mac and cheese, place macaroni mixture in a baking dish, sprinkle with bread crumbs, and bake at 350 degrees Fahrenheit for 15 minutes, or until crumbs are turning golden brown.

Another food that is now considered a soul food and/or southern dish is fried green tomatoes. This favorite Southern side can be found on many restaurant menus, perhaps because of its battered and hot oil, deep-fried appeal. Green tomatoes are merely a tomato that hasn't ripened. They are firm in texture and taste slightly tart or acidic. Given the contrasting flavors and textures, crunchy fried green tomatoes are often served with plump, juicy shrimp. Surprisingly, this is a relatively new dish that found its way into Southern kitchens after 1991's hit Fried Green Tomatoes. Most likely this recipe was adapted from Jewish immigrants who lived in the Northern states before becoming popularized by the movie. This knowledge inspired me to flip the script. Instead of making something crispy (as expected), I decided to make a simple creamy soup of roasted green tomatoes, paired with deliciously seasoned prawns. Followed later by a more traditional approach of frying the tomatoes and pairing them with another Southern favorite – pimento cheese.

FRIED GREEN TOMATO & PIMENTO CHEESE SANDWICHES

Estimated Time: 45 minutes
Servings: 6

Pimento Cheese Ingredients:

3 GREEN ONIONS, CHOPPED

1 TEASPOON OF ONION POWDER

½ TEASPOON GARLIC POWDER

½ TEASPOON SMOKED PAPRIKA

1/3 TABLESPOON LEMON JUICE

3 TABLESPOONS PIMENTOS, CHOPPED

½ CUP MAYONNAISE

1 ½ CUP SHARP CHEDDAR, SHREDDED

1 CUP MONTEREY JACK, SHREDDED

3 OUNCES CREAM CHEESE

Beat cream cheese with electric mixer until creamy. Add remaining ingredients and stir until well blended. Cover and refrigerate up to 7 days.

*time saver: I give you permission to substitute pre-made store bought pimento cheese if you're unable to make ahead. Sometimes you're busy and you need to cut corners to create a quick and delicious meal at home.

In a shallow dish combine breadcrumbs, flour, buttermilk powder, salt. Pepper, onion powder, garlic powder, and smoked paprika. You'll need to double batter the green tomatoes so next grab a bowl and beat eggs. Add water and hot sauce. Use a paper towel or lint-free towel to soak up moisture from tomatoes after slicing. Dip sliced tomatoes in egg mixture first to coat. Then flour mixture. Repeat the 2-step dredging process and shake off excess coating. Allow coated tomatoes to rest on a dry flat surface. Heat oil in skillet on medium. Gently lay tomatoes in hot oil and allow to brown 2 minutes or less. Once you see light brown around the edges of the tomatoes, flip over carefully and cook remaining side. Fry additional 60 seconds. Turn off heat and remove fried tomatoes with slotted spatula or tongs. Rest on paper towels and season to taste with a pinch of salt/pepper after removing.

CRISPY BUTTERMILK FRIED GREEN TOMATOES INGREDIENTS

3 LARGE OR 4 MEDIUM GREEN TOMATOES (SLICE ¼ TO ½ INCH THICK)

1 ½ CUPS PLAIN BREADCRUMBS OR PANKO

1 ½ CUPS FLOUR

¼ CUP BUTTERMILK POWDER (CAN BE FOUND NEAR DRY/POWDERED MILK IN STORES OR ONLINE)

1 TABLESPOON SALT

1 TEASPOON BLACK PEPPER

1.TEASPOON ONION POWDER

1 TEASPOON GARLIC POWDER

1 TEASPOON SMOKED PAPRIKA

1. TEASPOON HOT SAUCE

3 EGGS

3 TABLESPOONS WATER

VEGETABLE OIL, FOR FRYING

1 PACKAGE OF BRIOCHE BUNS (6 SANDWICH BUNS)

PIMENTO CHEESE

FRIED GREEN TOMATOES

SLICED RED ONION

BUTTER LETTUCE (6 LEAVES)

Assemble sandwich in this order:

1. Split brioche buns and add 3 heaping tablespoons pimento cheese on bottom buns.
2. Add green tomatoes.
3. Follow with lettuce leaf and red onions.
4. Top with bun.

Best served immediately after frying tomatoes. Tomatoes will be crisp and hot and a nice compliment to the pimento cheese, cool crunchy lettuce, and onions, covered by buttery soft buns.

ROASTED GREEN TOMATO SOUP

Estimated Time: 40 minutes
Servings: 6

1. Preheat oven to 450 degrees.
2. Spread tomatoes, onions and garlic on baking sheet and drizzle with 1 tablespoon olive oil.
3. Roast approximately 20 minutes until onions have caramelized, tomatoes are charred and the garlic is fragrant.
4. Sauté spinach with butter over medium-low heat until wilted.
5. Remove spinach from heat and add to high powered blender along with stock blend.
6. Add tomatoes and continue blending until smooth while slowly drizzling cream.
7. Taste soup after well blended and finish with olive oil, salt, and pepper.

Ingredients-

10 MEDIUM GREEN TOMATOES, CUT INTO QUARTERS

3 CUPS SPINACH

2 MEDIUM WHITE OR YELLOW ONIONS (CUT INTO QUARTERS)

5 GARLIC CLOVES, CRUSHED

3 TABLESPOONS OLIVE OIL

1/2 CUP HEAVY CREAM

1 CUP VEGETABLE BROTH

1 TABLESPOON BUTTER

PINCH SEA SALT

½ PINCH CRACKED BACK PEPPER

6-8 EDIBLE FLOWERS, OPTIONAL

SHRIMP & GREEN TOMATO SOUP

Estimated Time: 40 minutes
Servings: 6

Ingredients-

1-POUND EXTRA-LARGE, DEVEINED SHRIMP, TAIL-ON

2 TABLESPOONS MINCED GARLIC

1 TABLESPOON PARSLEY

1 TABLESPOON OLIVE OIL

½ CUP BUTTER

½ CUP WHITE WINE

1 LEMON, JUICED AND ZESTED

PINCH OF SEA SALT

1. Follow steps 1 – 3 above for soup.
2. In a separate pan, add olive oil.
3. Add shrimp (tails on) and cook 1-2 minutes per side. Remove shrimp when it's pink and just as it begins to look like the letter "C".
4. Add garlic in same pan. Cook 1-2 minutes, just until translucent.
5. Add wine, juice, and zest of ½ lemon.
6. After soup is finished blending, pour into bowls and serve with shrimp.

* Someone a long time ago, I don't recall who suggested I cook my shrimp and other seafood in its shells to enhance flavor. It does require extra work to remove before eating; however, the flavor is remarkable! "Don't take another mouthful before you have swallowed what is in your mouth." ~Malagasy Proverb

ROASTED LEMON BROCCOLINI

Estimated time: 20 minutes
Servings: 6

Ingredients-

1 ½ POUNDS BROCCOLINI

3 TABLESPOONS OLIVE OIL

1 ½ TABLESPOONS LEMON JUICE

2 TEASPOONS SALT

PINCH OF BLACK PEPPER

4 GARLIC CLOVES, MINCED

3 TEASPOONS GRATED LEMON ZEST

¼ CUP GRATED PARMESAN

---

1. Preheat oven to 450 degrees. Trim the bottom 2 inches off the broccolini stems and cut any thick stems in half so the stems are uniform/consistent in size.
2. Line a baking sheet with foil and lightly spray with cooking spray.
3. Add broccolini to pan and drizzle with olive oil, lemon juice and sprinkle with salt and pepper. Add garlic and toss until evenly coated. Line in a single layer making sure not to crowd or overlap pan.
4. Roast about 15 minutes until broccolini is your preferred tenderness. Remove from oven and toss with lemon zest and additional lemon juice if desired (taste first). Spread back into an even layer and sprinkle with Parmesan. Broil until Parmesan is melted, approximately 90 seconds. Continue to broil if you prefer a crispier or more charred dish. Season with additional salt and pepper to taste if desired.

CREAMED BRAISED MIXED GREENS

(similar to creamed spinach)
Estimated time: 30 minutes
Servings: 6-8

Ingredients–

6 TABLESPOONS BUTTER

2 SHALLOTS, SLICED THIN

4 CLOVES GARLIC, MINCED

1 CUP HEAVY CREAM

1 TABLESPOON COARSE SEA SALT

2-3 TEASPOONS SEASONING SALT

1 TEASPOON NUTMEG

4 POUNDS MIXED GREENS: COLLARDS, SWISS CHARD, MUSTARD, TURNIP OR KALE (ANY MIX OF THE AFOREMENTIONED). STEM GREENS AND SHRED.

TIP: For easy and consistent shredding of greens and herbs use a pizza cutter!

---

1. Heat 2 tablespoons of the butter over high heat until it begins to melt. As it begins to become frothy you'll notice a popping noise. This is because butter contains about 15%-17% water, so after a couple of minutes you'll see (and hear) tiny popping occurring in the saucepan. Don't be alarmed! Now reduce the heat to medium-low.
2. It's at this moment when you see the foam that you'll add the garlic and shallot stirring, until translucent (soft ened), about 5 minutes.
3. Add the cream next, bring to a simmer and cook until slightly thickened, 10 minutes.
4. Add the nutmeg and salt to taste. Using a hand blender, purée until smooth.
5. In a separate large pot, heat the remaining 4 tablespoons butter over high heat until it foams again.
6. Add the mixed greens, sauté, stirring constantly, until soft but still a bright green hue
7. after about 10 minutes sprinkle with salt, seasoning salt and add the cream mixture.
8. Lower the heat to low, cover and let simmer until cooked through, 5 minutes more.
9. Taste for nutmeg and salt, season to taste and serve hot.

BAKED TURNIP "FRIES"

Turnip fries are a great low-carb substitution for french fries. Prepare them as you would potatoes. Slice into wedges or french fry cuts and bake for a delicious alternative that can be eaten alongside sandwiches, burgers or served as a side.

Estimated Time: 45 minutes
Servings: 8

Ingredients-

1 TEASPOON ONION POWDER

1 TEASPOON GARLIC POWDER

1 TEASPOON SMOKED PAPRIKA

2 TEASPOONS SEA SALT

1 TABLESPOON OLIVE OIL

1 TABLESPOON PARSLEY

1/3 CUP PARMESAN CHEESE, GRATED

1. Preheat oven to 425 degrees.
2. Peel and cut turnips into ½ inch thick slices. Toss in oil and then add seasonings. Line baking sheet with parchment paper and lay fries in single layer. Bake 20-25 minutes. Remove and toss with parsley and parmesan. Taste for flavor. If salt is needed, add a pinch of sea salt.

AUTUMN HARVEST SWEET POTATO BISQUE

No peeling required. Just wash skin of produce and chop!

Ingredients-

As I mentioned before this soup is one of my all-time favorite soups to make… and eat! Based originally on the easy sauce I created while cleaning my fridge, not only is it rich and decadently creamy, but you'll be surprised at the ease of preparation. I can see this soup being served as a starter course for a nice dinner, but whenever I make it we never make it past anything else. Estimated time: 35 minutes

3 LARGE SWEET POTATOES, CHOPPED

2 BELL PEPPERS (RED, ORANGE OR YELLOW) CHOPPED

3 CLOVES GARLIC, CRUSHED

1 PEAR, CHOPPED (SUBSTITUTE GRANNY SMITH APPLE)

3 SPRINGS THYME

2 SPRIGS ROSEMARY

2 CUPS VEGETABLE STOCK (OR REDUCE TO 1 ½ IF ADDING WINE)

1 ¼ CUP HEAVY CREAM

¼ CUP WHITE WINE (OPTIONAL)

1 TABLESPOON COARSE SALT

1 TEASPOON CRACKED BLACK PEPPER

¼ TEASPOON NUTMEG

2 TABLESPOONS OLIVE OIL

---

1. Preheat oven to 400 degrees
2. Combine all produce in shallow baking pan and lightly toss in 1 tablespoon olive oil
3. Add thyme, rosemary to coat veggies before roasting
4. Roast 25-30 minutes until sweet potatoes and pear are soft and peppers and onions are softened and beginning to blister. Remove from oven and set aside
5. Move contents of pan into high-powered blender
6. Alternate adding vegetable stock, heavy cream and wine/liquid and blend 2 minutes until smooth
7. Add remaining olive oil, sea salt, cracked black pepper.
8. Blend additional 30 seconds and serve warm

BROWN BUTTER-POACHED COD WITH CAULIFLOWER PUREE AND ROASTED LEMON BROCCOLINI

This elegant dish sounds difficult to prepare but is surprisingly simple and looks stunning on a plate. If you're looking to impress someone with a date-night in, family meal, or just a delicious meal for one.

Estimated time: 10-12 minutes
Servings: 2

COD

Ingredients-

2 SMALL SHALLOTS CHOPPED FINELY
1 SPRIG ROSEMARY AND/OR THYME
2 SKINLESS DEBONED COD FILETS (RED SNAPPER ALSO WORKS WELL AND IS REASONABLY PRICED, HALIBUT IS A OPTION BUT CAN BECOME QUITE PRICEY)
½ CUP BUTTER

1. Preheat oven to 325 degrees.
2. Place your butter in a small saucepan (make sure it will fit both pieces of fish will fit – it should be tight) and heat over medium-low heat
3. After your butter has melted (after about 30 seconds), it will start to bubble and foam. Now When butter has melted, and water has evaporated out, the milk protein solids will begin to cook now.
4. As the foam begins to lesson, keep stirring and keep a close eye on the color of your butter. At this point it will become a light brown/amber color and it will smell delicious! A nutty aroma will consume your kitchen. Congratulations! You've just made brown butter!
5. Add the shallots at this point.
6. This next stage will go fast. Continue to stir a few more seconds. When you think the butter is a bit lighter than it should be, continue to stir, remove from heat and transfer butter to heatproof container.
7. After five minutes return butter to saucepan and gently lower cod into the warm butter, basting any exposed fish, and transfer to the oven. Cook for 3-4 mins, depending on the thickness of the fish, then turn the fillets over and cook for a further 3-4 mins or until just opaque and feeling firm
8. Estimated time: 10 minutes

CAULIFLOWER PUREE

Ingredients-

1 LARGE CAULIFLOWER HEAD, CHOP SMALL FLORETS

3 OUNCES CREAM CHEESE

2 TABLESPOONS SALTED BUTTER

3 CLOVES BLACK GARLIC, MINCED

1 TABLESPOON ROSEMARY, CHOPPED

---

1. Place a pot of water on medium heat
2. Add cauliflower florets to boiling water until fork tender
3. Remove from heat and drain after about 8-10 minutes
4. Place cauliflower and remaining ingredients in blender and blend until smooth and creamy

SHRIMP AND GRIT CAKES WITH CREOLE SAUCE

Ingredients-

4 TABLESPOONS UNSALTED BUTTER

¾ CUP WATER (AS NEEDED)

1 CUP WHITE CHEDDAR CHEESE, GRATED

½ CUP SMOKED GOUDA CHEESE, GRATED

BREADING

2 CUPS PANKO BREAD CRUMBS

4 EGGS

2 CUPS FLOUR

½ CUP CHOPPED PARSLEY OR GREEN ONIONS FOR GARNISH

SEASONED SHRIMP:

1 POUND JUMBO SHRIMP

1 LEMON PLUS ZEST

1 ½ TEASPOON CAJUN SEASONING

1 TEASPOON GARLIC POWDER

½ TEASPOON WHITE PEPPER

1 TEASPOON CREOLE MUSTARD

2 TABLESPOON BUTTER

1 TABLESPOON EXTRA VIRGIN OLIVE OIL

½ CUP HEAVY CREAM

1 TEASPOON CORNSTARCH

3 CRUSHED GARLIC CLOVES

How to make grit cakes:

1. Begin by whisking first four ingredients for grits in a pot over medium-high heat.
2. When mixture comes to a boil, lower heat, cover and simmer 30 minutes, whisking frequently to prevent clumps.
3. When grits are thick consistency but still creamy enough to stir smoothly, add butter.
4. Stir in cheeses and mix with a spoon until well incorporated.
5. Pour grits into a buttered casserole dish, cover and refrigerate overnight until set or for a minimum four hours.
6. Prepare the dredging station (a breading technique that involves dipping food into coating to retain foods moisture) by combining flour and panko together in one bowl then eggs into separate bowl.
7. Blend seasonings into panko blend and mix well.
8. Using a biscuit cutter, cut circles into grits. Place each "patty" in panko/flour mix and coat well, shaking off excess. Afterward, place patty in egg and coat well.
9. Repeat until all grit patties have been coated in each bowl.
10. Heat ½ cup of oil in a skillet over medium heat.
11. Place around 3 or 4 grit patties in the hot oil at a time and cook about 2 - 3 minutes per side until nice and golden brown. Remove from heat and drain.

How to prepare shrimp:

1. Rinse, peel, devein (remove intestinal track from shrimp), and season shrimp with all the seasonings, and squeeze a half lemon over shrimp. Mix well and let stand while you prepare sauce.
2. Melt butter then add olive oil over medium heat. Add crushed garlic and stir about 10 seconds. Add shrimp and cook about 3 or 4 minutes per side, depending on size of shrimp. If shrimp curls too tight and resembles the letter "O" you have overcooked it. It should resemble the letter "C" and be a pinkish color when it is cooked properly.
3. Remove shrimp to prevent cooking too long
4. Squeeze other half of a lemon, mustard, and cream to deglaze pan. Deglazing will help lift the bits of seasonings and flavor left behind by the shrimp. Stir until sauce has thickened,or if it does not begin to thicken, mix 1 tablespoon cornstarch with tablespoon water. This mixture is called a "slurry" and is used to help thicken sauces. *If mixture is too thick, add a neutral flavored liquid that will not dilute flavor such as a milk
5. Remove from heat after 5-7 minutes and continue stirring. Pour into gravy boat or serving dish to drizzle over grit cakes.

To assemble your grit cakes :

Place a couple tablespoons of sauce on the bottom of plate and top with a grit cake. Add more Creole sauce on top, then layer on another grit cake. Top with shrimp and more sauce if desired and garnish with green onions or parsley. Serve immediately

SMOKEY SHRIMP, ANDOUILLE SAUSAGE AND WHITE CHEDDAR GRITS

Estimated Time: 30 minutes
Servings: 4

Ingredients-

2 ANDOUILLE SAUSAGE LINKS, DICED (SUBSTITUTE BACON) 1 POUND EXTRA-LARGE SHRIMP, TAIL ON

4 GARLIC CLOVES, MINCED

½ LEMON

1 TABLESPOON PARSLEY

½ ONION DICED

½ RED BELL PEPPER, DICED

½ GREEN BELL PEPPER, DICED

2 TABLESPOONS SMOKED PAPRIKA (LIBERALLY SEASON SHRIMP)

2 TEASPOONS SALT

2 TABLESPOONS OLIVE OIL

Marinate shrimp first in olive oil, garlic, smoked paprika, salt, pepper for 30-40 minutes

1. Heat skillet over medium heat and a light drizzle of olive oil, then add diced sausages. Cook until browned and edges begin to darken (careful not to burn).
2. Add bell peppers and onions, sauté until onions are translucent.
3. Begin adding shrimp and marinade into ingredients, and stir.
4. Remove from heat after 2-3 minutes and leave shrimp in skillet until ready to serve.
5. Serve atop white cheddar grits (page 98) Follow instructions 1-4 for recipe.

Deah Berry Mitchell

Before receiving her master's degree in creative writing, Deah Berry Mitchell began researching the origins of soul food. She has worked professionally in the nonprofit development sector for over a decade, helping fundraise for a number of subjects ranging from higher education to health sciences. Hailing from Sherman, Texas, and like many Southern natives, she was raised in a family of traditionalists eating the very foods she's researched. After moving to Houston, Texas and gaining influences from various cultures, she began to incorporate those cooking styles into her recipes. Currently residing in Dallas, Deah founded a bus touring company and along with her business partner, educates the community about local black history contributions while marrying the influences of Black culture in the food scene.

When she's not developing recipes Berry Mitchell, a self-proclaimed food-enthusiast, enjoys traveling, entertaining friends and family at home, planning events and writing. Deah volunteers with local nonprofits, FEED Oak Cliff and Remembering Black Dallas, and works within the community to increase awareness of food and health equity.

References

Stephanie Smallwood, Saltwater Slavery:
A Middle Passage From Africa to American Diaspora (Cambridge: Harvard University Press, 2007), 34-35.)

"Slave Food." Encyclopedia of the Antebellum South. Santa Barbara:ABC-CLIO, 2000. Credo Reference. 2012

Cultural aspects of African American eating patterns. Ethnicity and Health, 1 (3), 245-60. Amenyenu, A., Tegegne, F., Singh, S. P., & Ekanem, E.(2010).

What We Eat. https://dcmp.org/series/162-what-we-eat. The Hand That Stirred the Pot

Robert L. Hall, "Africa and the American South: Culinary Connections," Southern Quarterly 44.2(2007)

Roseman JM. Diabetes in black Americans. In:
Harris MI, Hamman RF, eds. Diabetes in America. Bethesda, Md: US Department of Health and Human Services; 1985:1–24.

Centers for Disease Control and Prevention,
"Health Disparities Experienced by Black or African-Americans -- United States,"

"Differences in Disability Among Black and White Stroke Survivors --United States, 2000-2001,"

"Racial/Ethnic Disparities in Prevalence, Treatment, and Control of Hypertension -- United States, 1999-2002," MMWR, Jan. 14, 2005; vol 54: pp 1-3, 3-6, and 7-11

Admin, |. "African Crops and Slave Cuisine." The Sankore Griot. April 10, 2010. Accessed January 09, 2018. https://thesankoregriot.wordpress.com/2010/04/10/african-crops-and-slave-cuisine/.

www.ingramcontent.com/pod-product-compliance
Ingram Content Group UK Ltd.
Pitfield, Milton Keynes, MK11 3LW, UK
UKHW060118010826
14089UKWH00005B/49

9 781970 079135